VICTORIAN FAMILIES IN FACT AND FICTION

Also by Penny Kane

ASKING DEMOGRAPHIC QUESTIONS
(editor with David Lucas)
*CHINA'S ONE-CHILD FAMILY POLICY
(editor with Delia Davin and Elisabeth Croll)
CHOICE NOT CHANCE: A handbook of fertility control
(with Beula Bewley and Judith Cook)
THE CHOICE GUIDE TO BIRTH CONTROL
(with John Porter)
CONSUMER GUIDE TO BIRTH CONTROL
(with Margaret Sparrow)
DIFFERENTIAL MORTALITY: Methodological Issues and
Biosocial Factors
(edited with Lado Ruzicka and Guillaume Wunsch)
EHKAISY [Contraception]
*FAMINE IN CHINA 1959–61: Demographic and
Social Implications
THE SECOND BILLION: People and Population in China
SUCCESSFULLY EVER AFTER
(with Shirley Sloan Fader)
TRADITION. DEVELOPMENT AND THE INDIVIDUAL
(edited with Lado T. Ruzicka)
THE WHICH? GUIDE TO BIRTH CONTROL
*WOMEN'S HEALTH: From Womb to Tomb

**Also published by Macmillan*

Victorian Families in Fact and Fiction

Penny Kane

MACMILLAN

First published 1995 by
MACMILLAN PRESS LTD
Houndmills, Basingstoke, Hampshire RG21 2XS
and London
Companies and representatives
throughout the world

ISBN 0–333–61825–4

A catalogue record for this book is available
from the British Library.

10   9   8   7   6   5   4   3   2   1
04   03   02   01   00   99   98   97   96   95

Printed in Great Britain by
Antony Rowe Ltd
Chippenham, Wiltshire

This book is for my families – Maslins that were;
Forrester-Woods, Kanes, Ruzickas, Boltons and BB
that are – with love.

Contents

Acknowledgements

As usual, this book owes its existence to the encouragement and support of my husband, Dr Lado Ruzicka. His enthusiasm for the original idea, his painstaking reading and comments on the manuscript, have helped me immensely; he is not, of course, responsible for its remaining deficiencies. I am also grateful for the continuing encouragement of T. M. Farmiloe and Annabelle Buckley at Macmillan.

Introduction

The generalisations men accept about life, the morality which commends itself to them, are in some way reflected in the plays they see, in the songs they sing, in the stories they enjoy; and it is our duty as historians to try to understand that reflection.

G. Kitson Clark, 1962

During the nineteenth century, across Europe as well as in the United States, Canada, Australia and New Zealand, there was an extraordinary and quite unprecedented happening. People began to have fewer children, and went on having fewer children. It happened at slightly different times in different countries – in Britain, the fertility decline started around 1870 – but in each, it led to a reduction in the size of families which, with minor fluctuations, became and has remained a generally accepted norm.

Behaviour change on this scale is rare and unless there is some obvious immediate cause, such as a major technological development, very difficult to interpret. Why did people suddenly and simultaneously begin to feel that two, or three, children would be preferable to five or more? What had altered in their way of living and thinking which even put the possibility into their heads? This book is an attempt to suggest, through individual stories taken from biographies, letters and novels, some of the influences which might have impacted on our Victorian ancestors. At the same time I have tried to outline the broader demographic background which they were simultaneously creators of, and influenced by.

About people in the aggregate, demographers can tell us a great deal – for example, how many children were born, and to whom; when they married; how many children they had and at what ages; their life-span; where they lived and the jobs they had. A great deal of work has been done by demographers, too, in attempting to find explanations of why people behaved the way they did, by correlating the information about them with characteristics of their environment and society at large. Thus they can tell us that those who were in a higher social class, or had more education, married later or had smaller families. Or that miners and farmers changed their fertility behaviour later than people in other occupations.

One particularly elaborate effort to learn more about the declines in fertility in Europe was initiated by demographers at Princeton University. The Princeton Project has collected and analysed material about each of the seven hundred provinces or regions into which the European countries are divided. The Project has produced individual country studies as well as comparative ones; naturally, these have been a major source of ideas as well as data for this book, in addition to the work of British demographers.

Information about marriage, fertility, household size, longevity and so on is available for the whole of Britain for most of the nineteenth century. To learn about the earlier patterns of demographic phenomena, the special techniques of historical demography are needed. Much of what we now know is based on reconstructing family histories from parish records. Although the data are not as comprehensive as those taken from a census and modern vital registration systems, enough reconstruction has now been done in Britain – notably by the Cambridge Group for the Study of Historical Populations – to provide a reasonably comprehensive picture of demographic behaviour from the sixteenth century onwards.

The major limitation of demography, though, is that it does look at aggregates; it cannot tell us about the behaviour of individuals, let alone why they behaved as they did. For that, one has to learn individual stories and listen to individual voices. Using biographies and letters or diary-entries to explore the past is not unusual. Including novels as 'evidence' may need more explanation. When we read novels, we generally read for the plot, the characters, the language, the author's insight or wit; we tend not to notice consciously the small brush-strokes, the detail by which the novelist makes up his world. Nobody, for instance, reads *Madame Bovary* (Flaubert, 1857) for its description of the house of her wet-nurse. But the description is there; it is so detailed that you could draw a picture of that home; and it tells us a great deal about the conditions in which French children were expected to survive – if they could – and, implicitly, about how parents viewed children.

Novels are, in fact, a rich source of information about how people lived at the time, and what they thought. As historical sources of corroborative detail, 'do not overlook the novel', wrote Barbara Tuchman (1981), and she was right. I have been surprised and excited, trawling through nineteenth-century books, to see just how much there is about families and their relationships and conditions, as well as about love and marriage.

Inevitably, the question is, does a novel represent 'reality', and if so, to what extent? And I suppose the answer is that it depends at least partly on the author. At one end of the spectrum you have those like Gissing, who tried very hard to build a realistic setting for his stories by including a great deal of detail about the circumstances of the characters – often including the trivial, everyday events which other writers skim over.

At the other extreme are perhaps those like Emily Brontë, whose creations are simply but splendidly the product of a private world. *Wuthering Heights* (1847) is a wonderful book, but it would be difficult to accept that one could use it as an indication of the home life of most of Queen Victoria's subjects.

Other novelists wrote, quite deliberately, to make a point – to change attitudes or draw attention to an issue. These 'problem novels', as they were called, are usually well-grounded in fact but tend to intensify the facts to provide their own special pleading.

Yet others, like Dickens, use caricature or satire to heighten the points they wish to make, so that the result, while vivid, is slightly larger than life. The girls' school in *The Pickwick Papers* (1837) is a good example. It is not, in fact, an 'unrealistic' description; as we shall see, there were plenty of girls' schools, in fiction and in fact, which could easily have provided his model.

All the same, I have found it safer largely to avoid the problem novels and satire, and to concentrate on those writers who were only concerned to show a solid, recognisable background for their characters. Mrs Gaskell, George Eliot, and Trollope are examples. The selection of material glances back to the beginning, and forward to the end, of the nineteenth century, but I have focused mainly on books written or set between the 1840s and 1870s: the period immediately before and during the transition to smaller families.

Beyond that, my selection has not been based on any particular 'system'; undoubtedly, other novels could have been chosen which would have given similar or additional insights, and indeed I hope that those who are interested may be stimulated to re-read their own favourite Victorian writers from a new perspective.

One limitation – and it is a serious one – of any attempt to understand the past through what was written at the time is that the voices we hear are the voices of the literate, describing only those parts of society which they knew. Ford Madox Ford (1938) put his finger on the problem when he recalled his excitement at discovering D. H. Lawrence:

In the early decades of this century, we enormously wanted authentic projections of that type of life which had hitherto gone quite unvoiced. We had Gissing, and to a lesser degree Messrs H. G. Wells and Arnold Bennett. . . . But they all wrote – with more or less seriousness – of the 'lower middle' classes. The completely different race of the artisan – and it was a race as sharply divided from the ruling or even the mere white-collar classes as was the Negro from the gentry of Virginia – the completely different class of the artisan, the industrialist and the unskilled labourer was completely unvoiced and unknown.

Novels, letters and memoirs, then, may indeed offer insights about how some types and classes of people felt and behaved; they tell us much less about the habits of the working class. There were contemporary observers like Somerset Maugham, Arthur Morrison or George Moore, who were sharp-eyed observers of some aspects of working-class life. Their factual reporting of the way in which the poor lived is probably reliable. When it comes to the thoughts and emotions of their characters, let alone their reactions to any changes in their environment, however, such authors are less convincing. What we get is their interpretation, coloured and inevitably biased by the immense gulf of their experiences of life, so different to those of the working man. For me, these interpretations seldom ring quite true, and I have hesitated to use them, limiting myself instead to the more descriptive passages.

Because of the passage of time, we are even further from that world of 'the artisan, the industrialist and the unskilled labourer' than were Ford Madox Ford and the audiences of his period. We can do no more than guess how swiftly and how far the spread of education in the second half of the nineteenth century, and the development of cheap popular newspapers, may have helped to diffuse an awareness of some of the social developments of the times into working-class homes.

The growth of interest in oral history may do something to capture the stories of those 'ordinary' people who have survived from earlier generations. But how much can anybody who was only a child before the First World War, for example, tell us about their parents' attitudes to love and marriage – let alone sexuality? A child's partial world view, combined with the adult censorship of 'not in front of the children', limit the usefulness of what can be recalled about the particular topics which are the subject of this book.

Besides, as people grow older they adapt – to a greater or lesser extent – to the changes in their environment. They may forget or hide what they believed or did in an earlier age. My grandmother, married at the beginning of this century, frankly explained to a schoolfriend that she had accepted her husband because he had money and position. Writing her memoirs for her grandchildren, some sixty years later, she offered a more complex explanation.

> He was entirely unlike any other man who had been attracted to me before – 10 years older than I was and had quite a different outlook on life – but I was flattered and felt he had much to offer me: a lovely home – a settled way of life – and in some way his very difference attracted me.

Did she feel, in the 1960s, that she could no longer admit that it had been simply the 'marriage of convenience' which had still been an acceptable choice in upper-class Edwardian England? Or had she been more excited by his interest and his 'difference' than she felt able to confide to a young unmarried friend in 1904? We cannot tell.

And if we cannot be sure what even one individual thought, we certainly will never know with certainty what influenced all the people of Britain, let alone all the peoples of Europe and the European New World to make such a fundamental change in the size of their families. At best, if we listen carefully, we may get a few hints. This book is an attempt to listen.

1

Family Fluidity

One of the first things of interest about nineteenth-century families is that, as a consequence of population growth, there were rapidly increasing numbers of them. In 1801 the population of England and Wales was 8.9 million. By 1851 it was 17.9 million, and it grew to 22.7 million by 1871. Population expansion on such a scale was unprecedented, and the result was to produce a community of a completely different order to the one which had existed before the turn of the century.

Within that community, nineteenth-century families were – as in earlier times – fluid and unstable groupings, altered by frequent deaths and re-formed by new marriages. Family instability was something so widely accepted that people took it as normal and seldom commented on it. Probably just because it was so obvious as not to require explanation, it is easy for us today to overlook its significance. The mental picture we visualise when we think of the Victorian family – Mama, Papa, grandparents and innumerable children, solidly and placidly surrounded by mahogany and green baize – is, at best, a snapshot of a single moment; it is in many ways misleading.

In fact, few of those children would have known, for more than the briefest period, their grandparents. During the period 1838–54, life-expectation at birth was 39.9 years for men and 41.9 for women. After the 1860s it began to rise, and by 1901–12 reached 51.5 years for men and 55.4 for women (Teitelbaum, 1984).

Admittedly, these overall life-expectations do not give the whole picture. Where there is high infant and child mortality, those who survive beyond childhood are likely to live to greater ages than calculations of life-expectation at birth suggest. However, men and women who had survived to age 25 in 1901–5 could only be expected to live on average to just over 63 years (McKeown *et al.*, 1975), so it is reasonable to assume that throughout the second half of the nineteenth century many adults would die in their late fifties or at best, early sixties. Given that, as we shall see, the average age of marriage for women was above 25 during the same period, the

1

overlap of generations between grandparents and grandchildren was very small.

There was a further reason why grandparents were unlikely to be in the photograph of the family at home. Even if they were still alive, those of the older generation were not very likely to be living with their married children. Children in England had always, from as far back in the past as can be traced, left home to go and work elsewhere, or set up separate households when they got married (Laslett and Wall, 1972). In 1851, the census revealed that only four in every 100 households contained a parent of the household head, and only 12 contained grandchildren (Wall, 1983).

The chances of both Mama and Papa being in our imaginary family snapshot were also rather poor. A century ago in England, a sixteen-year-old marriage had the same chance of being broken by death as today it has of being broken by divorce (Holdsworth, 1988). Thus, a high proportion of children did not grow up in the presence of both their natural parents. About a third of households in the 1851 Census did not contain a household head together with a spouse (Wall, ibid.). Because women lived slightly longer, and generally married men who were a little older than themselves, it is probable that the majority of these household heads without spouses were women.

What the children very often had, instead of both their natural parents, was a step-parent – and also step-brothers and sisters. Two out of every five men across Europe in the nineteenth century who survived to age 50 had married and produced families more than once (Roussel, 1985). James Hill, father of the famous housing reformer Octavia Hill, for example, married three times and fathered one son and ten daughters. The boy and five of the girls grew up with stepmothers (Bell, 1942).

Stepmothers loom large in legend and tradition; sinister and malevolent, their treatment of the 'other' children of the family ranges from neglect to murder. The reality may have been less dramatic, but some sort of tension was probably inevitable. The gentle Molly Gibson, in *Wives and Daughters* (Gaskell, 1864–66), is heartbroken when her adored widower father breaks the news of his proposed remarriage.

> She did not answer. She could not tell what words to use. She was afraid of saying anything, lest the passion of anger, dislike, indignation – whatever it was that was filling her breast – should

find vent in cries and screams, or worse, in raging words that could never be forgotten. It was as if the piece of solid ground on which she stood had broken from the shore, and she was drifting out to the infinite sea alone.

Molly does not much care for what she has seen of the woman who will become her stepmother, but her anguish is at having to share her father with anybody.

The new Mrs Gibson is herself a widow, with a daughter. Although silly, hypocritical and totally self-centred, she is not intentionally unkind to Molly, nor does she discriminate (as she is fond of boasting) between the two girls.

Others may not have been so lucky. Trollope portrays a number of stepmothers, none of whom have much time for the daughters of their husbands' previous marriages. Typical enough is the case of Isabel Broderick, in *Cousin Henry* (1879), whose stepmother

had preferred her own babies to Isabel, and Isabel when she was fifteen years of age had gone to her bachelor uncle at Llanfeare.

When, after ten years, she returns to her father's house

It has to be acknowledged that Isabel was received somewhat as an interloper in the house. She was not wanted there, at any rate by her stepmother. . . .

Should the remaining parent die, the situation could obviously become more difficult. Soames Forsyte knows that Mrs Heron is a formidable ally in his determination to marry Irene despite her rejections of him over a two-year period:

His keen scent for the commercial side of family life soon told him that Irene cost her stepmother more than the fifty pounds a year she brought her; it also told him that Mrs Heron, a woman yet in the prime of life, desired to be married again. The strange ripening beauty of her stepdaughter stood in the way of this desirable consummation.

What had made her [Irene] yield he could never make out; and from Mrs Heron, a woman of some diplomatic talent, he learnt nothing. (Galsworthy, 1906)

Besides being brought into another family as the result of a remarriage, children were not infrequently adopted out of their original family, even when both their parents were still alive. In the second half of the eighteenth century, the Reverend George Austen had eight children to bring up on a limited income. His childless cousins, the Knights, began to invite his second son, Edward, for visits which became increasingly frequent and lengthy. George began to worry that young Edward was getting behind with his schooling, and wanted to keep him home. His wife said, 'I think you had better oblige your cousins and let the boy go.' The Knights eventually adopted Edward and made him their heir (Cecil, 1978).

Apart from the desire for an heir on the part of the childless Knights, they probably felt this was a practical way of helping the Austens financially. When George's daughter Jane grew up, she described a purely philanthropic inter-family adoption by the Bertrams (who have four children of their own):

> [Mrs Norris] could not but own it to be her wish, that poor Mrs Price should be relieved from the charge and expense of one child entirely out of her great number. 'What if they were among them to undertake the care of her eldest daughter, a girl now nine years old, of an age to require more attention than her poor mother could possibly give? The trouble and expense of it to them would be nothing compared with the benevolence of the action.' Lady Bertram agreed with her instantly. 'I think we cannot do better,' said she, 'let us send for the child.' (Austen, 1814)

When in 1840 Octavia Hill's father James lost his fortune, one of the daughters of his third marriage was adopted out by her maternal grandfather; this again was presumably to relieve the parents of financial expense. One result of the multiple marriages and their various progeny, as David Cecil (op. cit.) noted, was to confuse the generation levels.

> Aunts sometimes turn out to be as young as their nieces and stepsons the same age as their stepmothers.

Another result was that among the governing families of England, those who met each other daily in their various activities were, as Tuchman (1966) pointed out

> more often than not meeting their second cousins or brother-in-law's uncle or stepfather's sister or aunt's nephew on the other

side. When a prime minister formed a government it was not nepotism but almost unavoidable that some of his Cabinet should be related to him or to each other.

A further contribution to the fluidity of families was that children were particularly likely to die. That brood of children in our mental family snapshot were rather unlikely ever to have clustered around their parents simultaneously. Infant mortality in England and Wales in the middle of the nineteenth century was around 150 for every 1000 live births; and there was little significant change in the level until well after 1900. Throughout the period, between one and two out of every ten children died in their first year (Van der Walle, 1986). Those children who survived the first year were still very much at risk; in the second half of the century, in England and Wales, only three in the average family of four or five children might grow to adulthood (Ruzicka and Caldwell, 1977).

Of course, the statistics did not mean that every family was equally affected. Some, like Trollope's Mr and Mrs Toogood (1858), whom we shall meet later, would raise twelve healthy children; others, such as his miller Jacob Brattle (1870), would have twelve or fourteen and raise six. In general, the larger the families, the greater the likelihood of child losses – as is still true in many developing countries today – and the further down the social and economic scale a family were, the more children died – as is still the case everywhere.

The brood of children we pictured in the Victorian family snapshot was in any case seldom as large as we tend to imagine. Family size in England has, for several centuries, always been comparatively small. Between 1600 and 1800 completed family size fluctuated a little, but always averaged between five and six children per family (Wrigley and Schofield, 1983).

Overall fertility in Britain began its fall around 1870, and although the pace of the decline was uneven and varied in different regions, that date is generally accepted as marking the start of the 'demographic transition' in Britain. By around 1890, fertility had fallen by 10 per cent, which is the point at which demographers conclude that a change is not just a temporary fluctuation but an indication of real, long-term, shifts in behaviour. In other words, a noticeable – and ever-increasing – number of couples began having smaller families from 1870 onwards.

This change is nowhere reflected in the novels and memoirs from the late eighteenth century to the 1900s. From reading them it is possible to assume that families of two or three children were the norm among the British throughout the period. One reason for this, of course, is that any children who had died are not necessarily mentioned; thus the three children described may well be the survivors of, say, five who were actually born.

However, it is noticeable that – as we shall see in subsequent chapters – very large families are frequently singled out for comment, often with a distinct note of criticism. Most of the writers (especially in the earlier part of our period) were connected with the upper classes, which may have affected their views about family size. There do seem to have been class differences, both in Britain and elsewhere in Europe, in the number of children people had; the aristocracies, for example, show substantial falls in fertility between the seventeenth and eighteenth centuries, long before there is any similar trend in other groups (Livi-Bacci, 1986).

Among the surprising things about the fertility decline is that it took so long to spread beyond that small group at the top of society, given that Britain was the most highly industrialised country in the nineteenth century. By contrast, France had apparently adopted the concept of a smaller family from about the time of the Napoleonic wars (Knodel and van der Walle, 1986).

Another surprise is that when it did finally happen in Britain, the decline accelerated with amazing speed, compared with other European countries. From the first signs of a fall to that 'irreversible' 10 per cent decline it took only 16 years in England; in Germany it took 33 years (Watkins, 1986). Why the smaller family was so slow to spread initially, and caught on so rapidly, in Britain is still not explained.

A further puzzle is how couples managed to limit their family size once they had decided they wanted to do so, in the days before modern contraceptives. The rest of this book looks at some of the things which may have influenced the decline, and the ways it was brought about.

With regard to the timing of the decline, it should perhaps be remembered that the late 1860s and early 1870s produced a number of other changes which might have been expected earlier. The 1830s and 1840s had seen a major series of reforms, in the political and social fields, which were somehow not followed up. The historian Kitson Clark (1962) remarked that in the middle of the nineteenth century instead of a period of rapidly accelerating reform there seems to be a lull, a centre of indifference, an interlude of relative quiescence and indecision between the political activities of the first half of the century and the even more drastic changes that marked its close.

Those 'drastic changes' around the 1870s included the Reform Act of 1867 which further extended the franchise, notably in urban areas. Voting by ballot in parliamentary elections was introduced in 1872. Competitive examinations for entry into the Civil Service became general after 1870. Universal elementary schooling was introduced in 1870. It was only after 1867 that Dissenters were enabled to avoid paying Church Rates and in 1871 they became eligible for posts at the older universities. Flogging was abolished in the peacetime army in 1868, and the sale of commissions in 1871.

The important political shift which manifested itself in these developments, Kitson Clark argued, could not have happened overnight; it must have been something whose origins could be traced back to some earlier point in the century. Those apparently dormant middle years

> may be a period of social peace, and apparently of political stagnation, but is it possible that all the time powerful spiritual and social forces were at work under the surface which were changing the structure of society and preparing the way for the more obvious changes . . . ?

In the case of fertility decline too it is likely that powerful forces had been at work in the middle decades, preparing the way for the transition: many of those forces were very probably the same ones which changed other structures of society.

One of these 'powerful forces' was that families were ever more likely to find themselves in towns. Despite the growth in the overall population of England and Wales between 1841 and 1911, the size of the rural population hardly changed. The number of actual workers in agriculture declined by a quarter between 1851 and 1871 and by a further 35 per cent during the remainder of the century. During the same period the numbers of people in towns increased from 8.4 to 23.8 million (Teitelbaum, op. cit.).

The successive waves of migrants to urban areas created largely rootless, disconnected families. When John Bourcher, the strike-breaking weaver in *North and South* commits suicide, and his wife collapses at the news, it is neighbours, not relatives, whom Nicholas Higgins calls on to:

> 'each take a child with 'em, and to mind that they were orphans, and their mother a widow. It was who could do most, and the childer are sure of a bellyful today, and of kindness too.' (Gaskell, 1855)

Their widowed mother soon dies and Nicholas, unhappy at his own part in driving Bourcher to his death, takes on the six children: 'What are neighbours for?' The urban working-class extended family networks, so beloved by modern sociologists, had not yet had a chance to develop in cities with so many first-generation migrants.

The new job opportunities provided by the Industrial Revolution led to an expansion in the kinds of semi-skilled work which paid more than a farm labourer, for example, could expect. Working-class families benefited from these wider prospects, but they also benefited as consumers.

> As the century went forward, it produced even for poor people, if they had any money to spend at all, goods in a profusion and a variety which would have been beyond men's wildest expectations in earlier ages. The hastiness and carelessness of the manufacture of so much that was put on the market, the poorness in design, materials and workmanship which are often so painfully evident in what has survived, the silliness of a great deal of the reading matter which the new steam presses ran off, the obvious discomforts of a cheap railway excursion, may make one forget how much was being added to the richness of life. And when such things as washable clothes and soap are provided for those who would have had in the past little chance for such luxuries, the advantages to health and comfort are incalculable. (Kitson Clark, op. cit.)

Another development was the growth of what can loosely be called 'middle-class' families, and in particular families in the 'lower middle' class: represented by such people as clerks and retail shopkeepers. Defining the exact boundaries of that group is impossible, because some might have a smaller income than a working man or woman, while there may have been considerable differences between the lives and status of, for example, a law clerk and a commercial traveller, or a shopkeeper and his assistants. There seems, however, to be general agreement that the overall numbers of people who could be described as white-collar workers grew very rapidly during the century and especially in its second half. Not only did their numbers multiply but their proportion in the general population expanded very largely. In fact, a major reason for the Reform Bills of 1832 and 1868 was to appease the demands of the increasing – and increasingly insistent – numbers of those who did not belong to the nobility, gentry and established church and resented the stranglehold of those groups on power.

As the lower middle classes expanded, it seems that they also became more prosperous. The numbers of employees paying tax rose, and there was

a general progression up the ladder of income by the lower-salaried workers. . . . In the upper ranges there had developed a group who had managed to develop to a greater or lesser extent what might be called the apparatus of a gentleman such as additional servants, a trap or carriage, special education for their children. (Kitson Clark, op. cit.).

The same historian also points out that such families had not just become better-off. They had changed in more subtle ways.

They had become separated from the sympathies and class loyalties their parents had entertained and, as the third quarter of the century went forward, to an increasing extent they went to live in places remote from other classes and from the surroundings in which their parents had grown up. . . .

They were secure in their suburbs, and peer pressures came from others like themselves, upwardly mobile and ambitious, rather than from their families, childhood circle, or traditional sources of authority such as the local squire and his wife, or the vicar. There seems to be some evidence that it was these middle-class families who were to be the 'pioneers of family limitation' (Woods and Smith, 1983).

Charles Pooter, clerk and hero of *The Diary of a Nobody* (Grossmith and Grossmith, 1892), is a wonderful lower-middle class stereotype. He and his wife (who, incidentally, only have one child: the irrepressible Lupin) live in

'The Laurels', Brickfield Terrace, Holloway – a nice six-bedroomed residence, not counting basement, with a front breakfast-parlour.

Although Carrie is

> not above putting a button on a shirt, mending a pillow-case, or practising the 'Sylvia Gavotte' on our new cottage piano (on the three years' system) manufactured by W. Bilkson (in small letters) from Collard and Collard (in very large letters). . . .

and their sole servant is unpolished in the extreme, the Pooters think of themselves as gentleman and lady. They wear full evening dress for parties, to which the grocers supply champagne and port. The parties are attended by friends, not relatives: Carrie's mother lives in the country and is visited only for an overnight stay at Christmas. Church attendance is a badge of respectability – the Curate

> wants me to take round the plate, which I think a great compliment

reports Mr Pooter, who disapproves of Lupin wearing a check suit on a Sunday; but otherwise religion does not impinge upon their lives.

Although the middle classes grew rapidly, joining their ranks or rising through them was not a one-way process. Downward mobility was alarmingly frequent, and the fall could be dramatic. Bankruptcy is a pervasive theme in nineteenth-century fact and fiction. The economy lurched through many crashes as well as booms, and investment was far from secure. Recurrent and severe trade depressions were experienced between 1815 and 1832, while the remainder of the 1830s and 1840s were good times for industry, except during 1839–42, when there was a particularly severe depression. Despite some brief reverses and the shrinking of the agricultural sector, the good times continued or even intensified until 1876, which marked the beginning of the twenty-three year Great Depression. The Depression seems to have been uneven in its effects, with the middle classes suffering disproportionately (Teitelbaum, op. cit.).

Mr Thornton, Mrs Gaskell's (1855) wealthy Milton manufacturer, is the son of a man who had 'speculated wildly, failed and then killed himself'. Taken away from school to work in a draper's shop, he becomes the sole support of his mother and a sister too young to earn. Out of his earnings of fifteen shillings a week, his indomitable mother saves three, and eventually the young man – by instalments – manages to pay his father's debts, is taken in as partner by one of the creditors, and rises to being one of the greatest mill-owners. At the end of the book, however, he is only saved from another ruin by the newly-inherited wealth of the lady he loves.

Real life was no less subject to such dramatic booms and busts. James Hill – he of the three marriages and ten children – was the son of a long-established and wealthy family, and a banker whose firm was bankrupted in 1825. He made another fortune in corn and wool, and lost it in 1840; after struggling for a few years he finally collapsed, mentally and physically. His children were looked after by their maternal grandfather but, at the age of 13, Miranda, the eldest, became a pupil-teacher and as soon as she reached the same age, Octavia was put into a workshop to learn the business of something called 'consolidated glass', where she was also responsible for the stores. A year later she was put in sole charge of a toymaking business which employed Ragged School children (Bell, 1942).

At least Octavia, coming from an established family, had a grandfather who was able to help out for a time. Where upward mobility was recent it meant that a family might not have relatives in comfortable circumstances who would be able to assist, and financial disaster could reduce them quite literally to the life of paupers.

In addition to the inherent demographic, social and economic instability of nineteenth-century families, there was a kind of psychic fluidity as well. Novels and plays from the seventeenth century onwards very frequently featured foundlings, missing heirs and claimants, secret or fraudulent marriages, and unwittingly incestuous entanglements. In the nineteenth century such themes become increasingly common.

Parish-based registration of births, marriages and deaths had always largely excluded Catholics and Dissenters, and was increasingly ignored in the mushrooming cities where many of the poor did not consider themselves as belonging to any religious group. In 1836 civil registration was introduced, but was only partially observed. However, it did provide an opportunity for Dickens (1839) to make a joke about the propensity of women to lie about their ages:

... the daughter fourteen, as near as we can guess – impartial records of young ladies' ages being, before the passing of the new act, nowhere preserved in the registries of this country.

It was only when the onus of registering was transferred to the parents and fines for non-registration introduced in 1874 that vital registration became more or less universal (Glass, 1973). Meanwhile, increased population movements, especially to and from the New World, made it more difficult to check a person's antecedents; in many countries recording was, at best, erratic. For example, civil authority-based registration of vital events in Australia was introduced at different times by different states; Victoria (1853) and New South Wales (1856) were the last.

> Even then, it may be presumed that the records, particularly those from areas far remote from the urban centres, were incomplete. (Ruzicka and Caldwell, 1977)

Things were even more chaotic in the United States, where vital registration provisions varied from state to state and seem, in many, to have been a matter of indifference (Preston and Haines, 1991). 'There would be a certificate', says Paul Montague to the lady who claims that she has divorced her husband and that in any event he is now dead. Her scorn is apparent.

> 'Certificate; – in the back of Texas – five hundred miles from Galveston!' (Trollope, 1875).

Taking one typical Victorian writer – Trollope – and an almost random selection of his work, we find plots hinging on the legality of an Australian goldfields 'marriage' (*John Caldigate*, 1879); the status of an alleged American divorce (*The Way We Live Now*, 1875); and the difficulty for an apparently bigamous couple of proving the death of the wife's former, American, husband (*Dr Wortle's School*, 1881). Any of those plots seems reasonable, in the circumstances.

A similar vagueness about registration seems to have prevailed on the Continent. Osborne Hamley secretly marries in Metz, the ceremony being conducted by a travelling clergyman of his acquaintance, 'as good and blunder headed a fellow as ever lived'. Osborne assures his brother that he signed all manner of papers in the prefecture, though

'I did not read them over, for fear lest I could not sign them conscientiously . . .'

'But surely some registration or certificate was necessary?'

'Morrison said he would undertake all those forms; and he ought to know his own business. I know I tipped him pretty well for the job.'

'You must be married again,' said Roger, after a pause 'and that before the child is born.' (Gaskell, 1866)

Jane Eyre (Brontë, Charlotte, 1847) contains several examples of the difficulty of establishing who people were or whether what they claimed about their circumstances was true. Most memorable is the scene in which Jane is to be married to Mr Rochester, and the clergyman reads the part of the service about any impediment to the union:

He paused, as the custom is. When is the pause after that sentence ever broken by reply? Not once, perhaps, in a hundred years. And the clergyman, who had not lifted his eyes from his book, and had held his breath but for a moment, was proceeding: his hand was already stretched towards Mr Rochester, as his lips unclosed to ask, 'wilt thou have this woman for thy wedded wife?' – when a distinct and near voice said –

'The marriage cannot go on: I declare the existence of an impediment.'

The impediment is, of course, the first Mrs Rochester, married in the West Indies and, when Rochester has realised she is mad, brought back and hidden at Thornfield Hall. Because none of the local people know her identity, Rochester has no concern that the old traditional precaution of publicly reading the banns of marriage will expose his fraud. Only the chance that Jane has written to her uncle in Madeira, and that he talks to a brother of Mrs Rochester who is journeying back to the West Indies, uncovers the plot.

Other instances of the insecurity of identity in this novel include the failure of Jane's uncle to adopt her; when he makes the offer, Jane's guardian Mrs Reed, who hates her, simply informs him that Jane has died, and he accepts this without other evidence. Later, after the uncle has learned that Jane is alive after all, he leaves her his fortune, but she has disappeared and is hiding under a false name; only when she scribbles her real name unconsciously on a piece of paper does St John Rivers learn who she is – his cousin, the offspring of a marriage which annoyed her mother's family so much that there was no further contact between them.

In another example, *North and South* (Gaskell, 1855), Margaret Hale's brother is a naval mutineer who will be hanged if caught in England. Nevertheless, from his refuge on the Continent he is quite able to slip in and out, under a false name, in the days before official proof of identity was required in the form of a passport.

Michael Henchard, the Mayor of Casterbridge (Hardy 1886), sells his wife and child, Elizabeth-Jane, to a sailor. When they are reunited 20 years later, he accepts (in the absence of birth certificates) that the younger woman is his daughter; only his wife's deathbed confession admits that

> 'she died three months after that, and this living one is my other husband's. I christened her by the same name that we had given the first, and she filled up the ache I felt at the other's loss . . .'

When the sailor reappears in turn, Michael, for fear of losing the girl, claims that Elizabeth-Jane is dead. No proofs are required; the sailor just accepts the story. Only an accident finally reunites her with her natural father.

Concerns about the legality of marriages, the claims of heirs, and avoiding accidental incest, were inevitably largely limited to the respectable property-owning classes. The poor – at least the industrial poor – frequently did not bother to legalise their marriages at all, but, like Dandy Mick

> 'live in a two-pair, if you please, and has a wife and family, or as good' (Disraeli, 1845).

Mr Doolittle, in Shaw's *Pygmalion* (1916) thinks marriage entirely irrelevant, until his new prosperity forces him to wed his partner, a ceremony about which he is nervous.

> *Pickering*: But you've been through it before, man. You were married to Eliza's mother.
> *Doolittle*: Who told you that, Colonel?
> *Pickering*: Well, nobody told me. But I concluded – naturally –
> *Doolittle*: No: that ain't the natural way, Colonel: It's only the middle class way . . .

However, some of the poor did take the trouble to do things legally, as Ernest Pontifex discovers to his enormous relief, when it turns out that his 'wife', a drunken ex-servant, actually belongs to footman John who 'married her before the registrar at Letchbury on the 15th of August 1851' (Butler, 1903).

The continuing illiteracy of many of the working classes added to the difficulty of maintaining a cohesive family. Around the turn of the century, John Grout, the old farmer in *Akenfield* (Blythe, 1969), had worked on the railways in London.

There were lots of Suffolk men working there and hardly any mortal one of them ever got home again. They all wanted to get home, they were that sad in London. And their big wages were little there. Some ran away to Canada and were never heard of again. They couldn't write, you see; that is how they got lost.

In those years of agricultural depression, there were few chances of the men getting home: there were simply not enough jobs back in the village. But for those who could barely write, or who were quite illiterate, being away from home meant the gradual loss of all ties with their families – even if they did not go as far away as Canada. Among the millions who left Britain, during the nineteenth century and indeed even up to the First World War, a high proportion must have 'got lost' to their kith and kin.

2
Time and Thought

To live in England in the 1840s was an extraordinary, indeed a unique, experience. No other country had ever changed so fundamentally and so fast. The explosion of industry from the second half of the eighteenth century was accurately called a revolution, transforming the country and its people in a way hitherto unimaginable. Engels described the development of English manufacture, as he called it, in six breathless pages which still convey some of the contemporary excitement at the achievements; he summed up,

> a history which has no counterpart in the annals of humanity. Sixty, eighty years ago, England was a country like any other, with small towns, few and simple industries, and a thin but proportionately large agricultural population. Today it is a country like no other, with a capital of two and a half million inhabitants; with vast manufacturing cities; with an industry which supplies the world, and which produces almost everything by means of the most complex machinery; with an industrious, intelligent dense population, of which two-thirds are employed in trade and commerce, and composed of classes wholly different; forming, in fact, with other customs and other needs, a different nation from the England of those days. (Engels, 1845)

So extensive and all-embracing were the changes that affected people that it is extremely difficult to capture them all, and impossible in the context of this chapter, or this book. There is a vast literature on many aspects of the impact of industrialisation, on the way people thought about their lives and the world around them; for example, the spread of religious controversy and doubt, or the development of science and scientific principles. This chapter has a much narrower focus, on some of the concepts and controversies which had become sufficiently popular, or mainstream, to be reflected in the novels of the period. But it should never be forgotten that these particular concepts or controversies were only a small part of the immense upheaval which the industrial revolution brought to people's lives, especially in England where the pace and the extent of change were leading the world.

In the first half of the nineteenth century, in particular, England had an extraordinary power based not on war or empire but on its industrial triumph.

> I know of nothing more imposing than the view which the Thames offers during the ascent from the sea to London Bridge. The masses of buildings, the wharves on both sides, especially from Woolwich upwards, the countless ships along both shores, crowding ever closer and closer together, until, at last, only a narrow passage remains in the middle of the river, a passage through which hundreds of steamers shoot by one another; all this is so vast, so impressive, that a man cannot collect himself, but is lost in the marvel of England's greatness before he sets foot on English soil.

It was Engels again (1845) who wrote of this 'marvel of England's greatness' encapsulated in a view of the Thames. His words are a curious echo of Wordsworth (1807), who had seen from Westminster Bridge a scene differing only in its moment of brief tranquillity:

> Earth has not anything to show more fair:
> Dull would he be of soul who could pass by
> A sight so touching in its majesty:
> This City now doth like a garment wear
> The beauty of the morning; silent, bare
> Ships, towers, domes, theatres and temples lie
> Open unto the fields, and to the sky;
> All bright and glittering in the smokeless air.
> Never did sun more beautifully steep
> In his first splendour valley, rock or hill;
> Ne'er saw I, never felt, a calm so deep!
> The river glideth at its own sweet will:
> Dear God! The very houses seem asleep;
> And all that mighty heart is lying still!

Engels, of course, was a highly critical observer of what the industrial revolution had done to so many of its participants: indeed, the paragraph on England's greatness is followed by consideration of the 'sacrifices which all this has cost'; sacrifices which together make up the terrible indictment of *The Condition of the Working Class in England.* Nevertheless, he could not describe the achievement except in superlatives. The revolution's victims, too, saw it as something immense, superhumanly powerful:

> There is a King, and a ruthless King
> Not a King of the poet's dream;
> But a tyrant fell, white slaves know well,
> And that ruthless King is Steam.
>
> He hath an arm, an iron arm,
> And tho' he hath but one,
> In that mighty arm there is a charm,
> That millions hath undone
>
> Like the ancient Moloch grim, his sire
> In Himmon's vale that stood,
> His bowels are of living fire,
> And his children are his food ...
>   Edward P. Mead (1843)

The Steam King, like Wordsworth's 'mighty heart' was the creation of the new industrialists, men like the manufacturers of Mrs Gaskell's Milton in *North and South* (1854). The novel's heroine, Margaret Hale, is initially preoccupied with the lack of education or gentility among these manufacturers, but her first dinner party in the North reveals them to her in a different light.

> She liked the exultation in the sense of power which these Milton men had. It might be rather rampant in its display, and savour of boasting; but still they seemed to defy the old limits of possibility, in a kind of fine intoxication, caused by the recollection of what had been achieved, and what yet should be. If in her cooler moments she might not approve of their spirit in all things, still there was much to admire in their forgetfulness of themselves and the present, in their anticipated triumphs over all inanimate matter at some future time which none of them should live to see.

That optimistic sense of unlimited possibility was founded on the undeniable fact that the dominion of the possible was being extended all the time. It enthused Harry Clavering, a Trollope hero, to the ambition to become an engineer, rather than enter the church as his background dictates and his family wishes.

> 'You see I could have no scope in the church for that sort of ambition which would satisfy me. Look at such men as Locke, and Stephenson, and Brassey. They are the men who seem to me to do most in the world. They were all self-educated, but surely a man can't have a worse chance because he has learned something. Look at old Beilby with a seat in Parliament, and a property worth two or three hundred thousand pounds! When he was my age he had nothing but his weekly wages.'
>
> 'I don't know whether Mr Beilby is a very happy man or a very good man,' said Mary.
>
> 'I don't know either,' said Harry; 'but I do know that he has thrown a single arch over a wider span of water than was ever done before, and that ought to make him happy.' (Trollope, 1867)

Torn between two different women, Harry has little time to apply himself to engineering; ultimately he is fortunate enough to come into an inheritance and gives up the dream which was always, for him, inappropriate. All the same, his ambition shows that he had sensed the inner satisfaction with which Kipling's bridge-builder Findlayson looks at his almost completed span across the Ganges; a bridge which has changed the face of the country for seven miles around:

> Looked back on the humming village of five thousand workmen; up-stream and down, along the vista of spurs and sand; across the river to the far piers, lessening in the haze; overhead to the guard-towers – and only he knew how strong those were – and with a sigh of contentment saw that his work was good. There stood his bridge before him in the sunlight, lacking only a few weeks' work on the girders of the three middle piers – his bridge, raw and ugly as original sin, but *pukka* – permanent – to endure when all memory of the builder, yea, even of the splendid Findlayson truss, had perished. (1898)

Findlayson does not only build bridges where none could have been built before; he is an inventor ('the Findlayson truss') who finds new or improved ways to achieve the impossible. Invention, or discovery, were in the air, so that even a young country doctor could dream of extending the boundaries of science. The young Lydgate, in *Middlemarch* (Eliot, 1872), accidentally picked up a volume on anatomy:

> A liberal education had of course left him free to read the indecent passages in the school classics, but beyond a general sense of secrecy and obscenity in connection with his internal structure, had left his imagination quite unbiased, so that for anything he knew his brains lay in small bags at his temples, and he had no more thought of representing to himself how his blood circulated than how paper served instead of gold. But the moment of vocation had come, and before he got down from his chair, the world was made new to him by a presentiment of endless processes filling the vast spaces planked out of sight by that wordy ignorance he had called knowledge.

He determines to become a country general practitioner, a modern and reforming one who will

> win celebrity, however slowly, as Jenner had done, by the independent value of his work.

But, still in the footsteps of Jenner, he is also

> ambitious of a wider effect: he was fired with the possibility that he might work out a proof of an anatomical conception and make a link in the chain of discovery.

The 'chain of discovery' was seen as a general process feeding the unstoppable March of Progress. It was open to everybody with intelligent observation to forge one of its links, in any sphere.

The bridge for which Findlayson had designed his trusses was built to carry a railway. Railways were a popular topic for novelists, perhaps partly because of their visibility as a symbol of the modern. Thus the conservative Lady Dunstane in the 1850s, at a time when railway-fever was sweeping England, could only reflect:

> Those railways! When would there be peace in the land? Where one single nook and shelter and escape from them! And the English, blunt as their senses are to noise and hubbub, would

be revelling in hisses, shrieks, puffings, and screeches, so that travelling would become an intolerable affliction. . . .

She complains to her friend Redworth, who has invested everything he owns in railway shares, that

'. . . this mania for cutting up the land does really cause me to pity those who are to follow us. They will not see the England we have seen. It will be patched and scored, disfigured . . .'.

Redworth is unrepentant:.

'Simplicity must go, and the townsman meet his equal in the countryman. As for beauty, I would sacrifice that to circulate gumption. A bushelful of nonsense is talked pro and con; it always is at an innovation. What we are doing now is to take a longer and quicker stride – that is all.' (Meredith, 1885)

One Englishman who did revel, as Lady Dunstane had forecast, in the 'hisses, shrieks, puffings and screeches' was Trollope. Awed by the spectacle which such places presented, he wrote of 'Tenway' Junction:

a marvellous place. . . . The space occupied by the convergent rails seems to be sufficient for a large farm. And these rails always run one into another with sloping points, and cross passages, and mysterious meandering sidings, till it seems to the thoughtful stranger to be impossible that the best trained engine should know its own line. Here and there and around there is ever a wilderness of wagons, some loaded, some empty, some smoking with close-packed oxen, and others furlongs in length black with coals, which look as though they had been stranded there by chance, and were never destined to get again into the right path of traffic. Not a minute passes without a train going here or there, some rushing by without noticing Tenway in the least, crashing through like flashes of substantial lightning, and others stopping, disgorging and taking up passengers by the hundreds . . . over all this apparent chaos there is presiding a great genius of order. (Trollope, 1876)

For the suicide of his Heathcliffian character Ferdinand Lopez, no setting could be more dramatically fitting.

There came a shriek louder than all the other shrieks, and the morning express down from Euston to Inverness was seen coming round the curve at a thousand miles an hour. Lopez turned round and looked at it . . . with quick, but still with gentle and apparently unhurried steps, he walked down before the flying engine – and in a moment had been knocked into bloody atoms. (Trollope, ibid.)

If Redworth thought the coming of the railways involved only a longer and quicker stride into the future, others made greater claims. Stephen Morley, the Chartist journalist in *Sybil*, believed that

'the railways will do as much for mankind as the monasteries did' (Disraeli, 1845)

and Kipling, in *William the Conqueror*, a story about the successful containment of an Indian famine, described the trains carrying grain the length and breadth of the country to reach starving villagers, who have been moved – also by train – into camps so that the food can be distributed easily. In *The Bridge-Builders*, however, he noted that trains help to spread epidemics. That story used the coming of Findlayson's bridge as a kind of metaphor for industrialisation, or modernisation, which Kipling saw overturning the entire belief-system of the past.

A great flood threatens the unfinished bridge; Findlayson, worn out with his efforts to avert disaster, is given opium by his Indian assistant Peroo. The two are swept by the flood on to an island, refuge from the water for the birds and beasts who represent the Gods of India. The two men listen to them discussing what the bridge and all it encapsulates means to them, and whether it should be destroyed. Some agree with Kali, Goddess of Destruction, that the people

'will see that Mother Gunga can avenge no insult, and they fall away from her first, and later from us all, one by one. In the end, Ganesh, we are left with naked altars . . .'.

Hanuman the Ape argues that it will only be the names of the gods that change, not their worship:

'I have made a man worship the fire-carriage as it stood still breathing smoke, and he knew not that he worshipped me . . .

they will do no more than change the names, and that we have seen a thousand times.'

But Krishna tells them that they are, indeed, finished.

'Drink now and eat greatly! Bathe your faces in the smoke of the altars before they grow cold! . . . As men count time the end is far off; but as we who know reckon it is today.'

When the men wake, Findlayson can recall only that the island was full of beasts and men talking. He is quite indifferent to their topic, and indeed to the magical reality that the animals did talk. Paroo is reminded of a time when he was almost lost overboard at sea, and abandoned prayer in order simply to hold on: to rely on his own strength. He says

'Then it *is* true . . . When Brahm ceases to dream, the Gods go.'

The Gods, or some of them, had already begun to disappear in England. The gradual discovery of the links of chains of causation which led to sickness and death, for example, undermined the belief in arbitrary fates, and of the desirability of helpless submission to them.

The fatal illness of Margaret Hale's mother forces the Milton doctor to admit that

'. . . we cannot touch the disease, with all our poor vaunted skill. We can only delay its progress – alleviate the pain it causes. Be a man, sir – a Christian. Have faith in the immortality of the soul, which no pain, no mortal disease, can assail or touch!' (Gaskell, 1855)

The doctor accepts, though he plainly regrets, his impotence. Others thought that efforts to combat disease were in themselves wicked. William Lovett (1876), born in the Cornish fishing town of Newlyn in 1800, remembered catching smallpox as a child.

Vaccination at that time had not been introduced into our town, though inoculation for the small-pox was occasionally resorted to; but it was looked upon as sinful and a doubting of providence, although about that period one in every fourteen persons born died from its ravages.

Some forty years later, Kingsley (1857) depicts the Cornish as having changed little in their attitude to epidemics. When the old doctor in the fictitious town of Aberalva is warned of an approaching cholera epidemic, and urged to get his patients to clean up their homes he refuses, on the grounds that he will only offend them,

> 'And all on the chance of this cholera coming, which I have no faith in, nor in this new-fangled sanitary reform neither, which is all a dodge for a lot of young Government puppies to fill their pockets, and rule and ride over us: and my opinion always was with the Bible, that 'tis jidgment, Sir, a jidgment of God, and we can't escape His holy will, and that's the plain truth of it.'
>
> Tom made no answer to this latter argument. He had heard that ' 'tis jidgment' from every mouth . . .

When the cholera duly arrives, the apparently random pattern of deaths hardens

> the hearts of fools by fresh excuses for believing [it] had nothing to do with drains and water; that [it] was 'only' – such an only! – 'the Visitation of God.'

The Cornish were not alone in their fatalism. In March 1832, the Government's response to a cholera epidemic had been to decree a national day of fasting to beg God to remove the scourge. Lovett (1876) commented tartly that, having become convinced that most of the ravages of cholera were due to want and wretchedness in the slums, he and his fellow-workers thought any additional fasting was the last possible thing those poor creatures needed.

> We believed also that the causes that matured and extended that disease were greatly within the power of Government to remove; and, therefore, saw in this proposed fast an attempt on the part of rulers to father their own iniquitous neglect upon the Almighty.

Twenty years later there was another major cholera epidemic – the one whose impact in Aberalva Kingsley described. This time, the Government responded very differently. From the Scots, who – as Buckle (1861) described them – were

> moved by that dire superstition which sits like an incubus upon them

came demands for a religious fast

> which, in so superstitious a country, was sure to be rigidly kept, and, being rigidly kept, was sure to enfeeble thousands of delicate persons, and, before twenty-four hours were passed, prepare them to receive that deadly poison which was already lurking around them, and which, hitherto, they had just strength enough to resist. The public fast was also to be accompanied by a public humiliation, in order that nothing might be wanting to appal the mind and fill it with terror. . . . The Scotch clergy took it for granted that the cholera was the result of Divine anger, and was intended to chastize our sins.

Palmerston, the Prime Minister of the time, refused to invoke the Church. Instead, he pointed out that the world was ruled by natural laws, and one of those was that disease resulted from dirt. He told the Scots to clean up their slums, freeing them

> from those causes and sources of contagion which, if allowed to remain, will infallibly breed pestilence, and be fruitful in death, in spite of all the prayers and fastings of a united, but inactive nation. (Buckle, ibid.)

To some extent, this very different reaction may have reflected differences in character between the two politicians: the feeble Spencer Percival in 1832 and the cool rational Palmerston in 1853. But it also reflected an increased understanding of the 'natural laws' which ruled the world. That understanding was not necessarily comprehensive. Palmerston, like Kingsley, was presumably a believer in the 'modern' theory that cholera, along with many other diseases, was caused by a miasma – infection carried in foul air. The role of microbes had not yet been discovered. Nevertheless, the observations which led to miasmic theory were basically sound. Dirt did breed pestilence, and efforts to improve hygiene reduced its impact.

Reliance on the existence of natural laws, and on being able to discover and make use of them if one made the effort, were behind Lydgate's dream of 'making a link in the chain of discovery' and the Milton manufacturers' confidence in 'ultimate triumph over all inanimate matter'. Such confidence also upheld Tom Thurnall, FRCS, shipwrecked on the Cornish coast in time to help fight the cholera at Aberalva. Tom was an enthusiastic scientist who supplemented his earnings by mounting biological specimens for sale. Elsley Vavasour, puzzled as to why anybody would pay for 'a bit of dirt', is shown a zoophyte under a microscope

> and beheld a new wonder – a living plant of crystal, studded with crystal bells, from each of which waved a crown of delicate arms.
>
> 'This is most beautiful,' said he at length.
>
> 'Humph! why should not Mr Vavasour write a poem about it?'
>
> 'Why not, indeed?' thought Elsley.
>
> 'It's no business of mine, no man's less: but I often wonder why you poets don't take to the microscope, and tell us a little more about the wonderful things which are here already, and not about those which are not, and which, perhaps, never will be. . . . This little zoophyte lives by the same laws as you and I; and . . . he and the seaweeds, and so forth, teach us doctors certain little rules concerning life and death . . .'. (Kingsley, 1857)

The conviction that man had the ability to discover and use natural laws, although it undoubtedly speeded the pace of scientific development, seems to have arisen as much from a general climate of thought as from particular discoveries or innovations.

So, at least Kipling seems to imply, in a story which suggests that knowledge at the wrong time may be useless or even dangerous. 'The Eye of Allah' is set in an abbey at the time of the Crusades, where there is much discussion of healing, and of the causes of disease. To the abbey, the artist John of Burgos brings a Moorish *ars optic* – a magnifying-glass, the 'eye' of the title. The surgeon, Roger of Salerno, looks through it at a drop of dirty water and

> . . . stepped back at last, as though stricken.
>
> 'It is a new world – a new world – and – Oh, God Unjust! – I am old!'
>
> . . . John manipulated the tube for the Infirmarian, whose hands shook, and he too looked long.
>
> 'It is Life,' he said presently in a breaking voice. 'No hell! Life created and rejoicing – the work of the Creator!'

The little group realises the scientific importance of what they have seen. But the Abbot knows that the Church, fearing heresies and divisions, is in witch-hunting mood. He knows too that such an instrument, brought from the Islamic world, will show most people

'a hell of devils contending in the compass of one drop of water. Magic past utterance! ... this birth, my sons, is untimely. It will be but the mother of more death, more torture, more division, and greater darkness in this dark age.' (Kipling, 1926)

Taking the action upon his own conscience, he breaks the instrument in pieces, trusting that a more enlightened age will value and make use of its potential.

Scientific thinking, in a more general sense, could arise from the very process of industrialisation. Joe Scott, foreman of a Yorkshire cloth-mill, is proud of his reasoning powers:

'... mechanics like me is forced to think. Ye know, what wi' looking after machinery and suchlike, I've getten into that way that when I see an effect, I look straight out for a cause, and I often lig hold on't to purpose; and then I like reading, and I'm curious to knaw what them that reckons to govern us aims to do for us an wi' us. And there's many 'cuter nor me ...'. (Brontë, Charlotte, 1849)

Joe believes both in his ability to deduce scientific cause from effect, and in his right to extend that ability to broader matters of politics and government. He has moved as far from the superstitions and deference of the traditional village as has his master, Robert Moore, from the classic conservatism of the ruling classes. Reproached by his vicar, the embodiment of such conservatism, for his revolutionary ideas, Moore retorts:

'I can think what I please, you know ... both about France, and England; and about revolutions, and regicides, and restorations in general; and about the divine right of kings ...'. (Brontë, Charlotte, 1849)

He rejected the claim that kings govern by divine right; indeed, he disapproved of kings. Bonaparte, as the leader of revolutionary France, had been his hero; the Emperor Napoleon his despair. Robert Moore's ideas stem from the liberal Enlightenment of the eighteenth century; from the French Encyclopaedists, American revolutionaries and the England of Hume, Gibbon and Tom Paine. None of them, however, interferes with his capitalist drive; he has (until softened by love) little sympathy for his struggling workforce, and pursues with ruthless vengeance those Luddite leaders who try to destroy the mills and their machines. He is, in addition, scornful of Joe's militant working-class philosophy.

Joe Scott and Robert Moore between them represent the two strands of influence which combined to form the increasingly sceptical and rationalist values of the nineteenth century. Such values inevitably conflicted with the comfortable world of the Established Church which, in Trollope's Barchester novels, is already under siege. One reason was that churchmen of that type seemed increasingly inappropriate. By the 1880s Lady Aurora Langrish, in *The Princess Casamassima*, is discussing them with frank distaste. She is quick to reject the suggestion that she is very religious, even though in her nature charity exists as 'a kind of passion'.

> 'I don't know. One has one's ideas. Some of them may be strange. I think a great many clergymen do good, but there are others I don't like at all. I dare say we had too many always at home; my father likes them so particularly. I think I've known too many bishops, I've had the church too much on my back.' (James, 1886).

Some took refuge in nonconformism. The Census of religious worship in England and Wales in 1851 found that, among the churchgoers, almost half – 48 per cent – chose to go elsewhere than the Church of England; there was thus a very large body of worshippers who were looking for a different sort of spiritual inspiration from that offered by the establishment.

The religious Census also found that fewer than 7.3 million of the 17.9 million people in the country went to church at all on the Sunday in question. Even those who did go were increasingly affected by doubt. Thus a young man like George Bertram in *The Bertrams*, having abandoned his legal studies, and being in urgent need of making a name and some money, could do both by writing a controversial book on religion.

> The name of his little book was a very awful name. It was called the *Romance of Scripture*.

The book questioned literal belief in the Bible, arguing that its authors wrote in ignorance of those natural truths which man had now acquired by experience and induction, and not by revelation. Their truth was the truth of heaven, not the truth of earth. No man thought that the sun in those days did rise and set, moving around the earth, because the prolongation of the day had been described by the sun standing still upon Gibeon . . .

The book was undoubtedly clever, and men read it. Women also read it, and began to talk, some of them at least, of the blindness of their mothers who had not had wit to see that these old chronicles were very much as other old chronicles. (Trollope, 1859)

Bertram writes a second book, in which he goes further, by using the words 'myth' and 'mythical' about many Biblical accounts of events; as a result he is made to resign his Fellowship at Oxford. His old friend Arthur, who is a vicar, reproaches him for going into matters which are not vital to faith in the Christian religion, but Bertram answers,

> 'What is vital, and what is not? If I could only learn that! But you always argue in a circle. I am to have faith because of the Bible; but I am to take the Bible through faith.'
> 'If every man and every child is to select, how shall we ever have a creed? and if no creed, how shall we have a church?'
> . . . . . 'In these days men do not even know what faith is.'

Many had become willing to admit that they had no faith. People who did not attend any place of worship on that Census Sunday in 1851 were divided by contemporaries into those who were given up to 'low sensual indulgence' and those who were 'marked by a sceptical activity of mind, disposed to question everything' (Kitson Clark, 1962).

That latter group were artisans and working men, great readers, class-conscious, keen to be able to vote and inclined to atheism. Mrs Gaskell's *North and South* (1855) has an affectionate portrait of a fairly typical specimen in Nicholas Higgins, whom we meet in other chapters of this book. Another of these unabashed atheists is a tinker, Mr Shaw. Ernest Pontifex, just out of university and inspired by revivalism, tries to convert him. Ernest

led the conversation to Whateley's *Historic Doubts* – a work which as the reader may know pretends to show that there never was any such person as Napoleon Bonaparte, and thus satirises the arguments of those who have attacked the Christian miracles.

Mr Shaw replied that he knew *Historic Doubts* perfectly well.

'And what do you think of it?' said Ernest, who regarded the pamphlet as a masterpiece of wit and cogency.

'If you really want to know,' said Mr Shaw with a sly twinkle, 'I think that he who was so willing and able to prove what was, was not, would be equally willing and able to prove that what was not, was, if it suited his purpose.'

Ernest was very much taken aback. How was it that all the clever people at Cambridge had never put him up to this simple rejoinder? The answer is easy: they did not develop it for the same reason that a hen had never developed webbed feet – that is to say because they did not want to do so – but this was before the days of Evolution, and Ernest could as yet know nothing of the great principle that underlies it. (Butler, 1903)

The 'great principle' of evolution, advanced in 1859, further undermined faith in the literal truth of the Bible. Twenty years later, the theory was known to everybody – at least in outline. Nancy Lord is the daughter of a dealer in pianos, living in Camberwell.

Nancy was no longer inclined to study, and cared little for reading of any sort. That new book on Evolution, which she had brought from the library just before Jubilee Day, was still lying about; a dozen times she had looked at it with impatience, and reminded herself that it must be returned. Evolution! She already knew all about Darwinism, all she needed to know. If necessary she could talk about it – oh, with an air! (Gissing, 1894)

The spread of education – discussed in another chapter – had produced, among the ranks of the lower middle classes, artisans and working men, many who could talk about all sorts of topics 'with an air'. Nancy's father has taken a young man into partnership: Samuel Barmby, son of a nonconformist insurance clerk.

Samuel conceived himself much ahead of his family. Quite uneducated in any legitimate sense of the word, he had yet learned that such a thing as education existed, and, by dint of busy perusal of penny popularities, had even become familiar with names and phrases, with modes of thought and ambition, appertaining to a world forever closed against him. He spoke of Culture, and imagined himself far on the way to attain it. His mind was packed with the oddest jumble of incongruities; Herbert Spencer jostled with Charles Bradlaugh; Matthew Arnold with Samuel Smiles; in one breath, he lauded George Eliot, in the next, was enthusiastic over a novel by Mrs Henry Wood; from puerile facetiae he passed to speculations on the origin of being, and with equally light heart. (Gissing, 1894)

Charles Bradlaugh, lying among the 'jumble of incongruities' in Samuel's mind was, among other things, a leading advocate of birth control, as is described in a later chapter. One wonders whether that idea, too, had lodged in Samuel's brain. Certainly, Malthus and his theory that population growth always tends to outstrip the food supply was sufficiently well-known for Dickens to refer to it in *A Christmas Carol* (1843). The unregenerate Scrooge is quite content to let the suffering poor die, for it will 'decrease the surplus population'.

A few years later, Malthus has become an undergraduate joke. Frank Gresham explains to his aunt that

'I am to take my degree in October, aunt; and I am determined, at any rate, that I won't be plucked [failed].'

'Plucked!'

'No; I won't be plucked. Baker was plucked last year, and all because he got into the wrong set at John's. He's an excellent fellow if you know him. He got among a set of men who did nothing but smoke and drink beer. Malthusians, we call them.'

'Malthusians!'

' "Malt", you know, aunt, and "use"; meaning that they drink beer.' (Trollope, 1858)

By the end of the century, however, it is the concerns of the geneticists, rather than those of Malthus, of which we catch an echo. A local surgeon in *A Child of the Jago* has been into a festering East End slum to deliver a baby, and wonders if its survival is a matter for congratulation:

'Is there a child in all this place that wouldn't be better dead – still better unborn? But does a day pass without bringing you such a parishioner? Here lies the Jago, a nest of rats, breeding, breeding, as only rats can; and we say it is well . . .'

Father Sturt walked a little way in silence. Then he said: 'You are right, of course. But who'll listen, if you shout it from the housetops? I might try to proclaim it myself, if I had time and energy to waste. But I have none – I must work, and so must you. The burden grows day by day, as you say. It's hopeless, perhaps, but that is not for me to discuss. I have my duty.'

The surgeon was a young man, but Shoreditch had helped him over the most of his enthusiasms. 'That's right,' he said, 'quite right. People are so very genteel, aren't they? . . . Think how few men we trust with the power to give a fellow creature a year in gaol, and how carefully we pick them! Even damnation is out of fashion, I believe, among theologians. But any noxious wretch may damn human souls to the Jago, one after another, year in year out, and we respect his right: his sacred right.' (Morrison, 1896)

Morrison's horror at the 'noxious wretches' of the Jago did not make him any more sympathetic to attempts to uplift the East Enders. He scorns the burgeoning number of Literary Institutes, Working Men's Institutes and other efforts to bring literacy and education to the working classes. The tone of patronising contempt with which Morrison writes of worker's educational schemes reflects Gissing's distaste for Samuel's struggles at self-improvement:

The triumphs of the East End Elevation Mission and Pansophical Institute were known and appreciated far from East London, by people who knew less of that part than of Asia Minor. Indeed, they were chiefly appreciated by these. There were kept, perpetually on tap for the East Ender, the Higher Life, the Greater Thought, and the Wider Humanity: with other radiant abstractions, mostly in the comparative degree, specifics all for the manufacture of the Superior Person. There were many Lectures given on still more subjects. Pictures were borrowed and shown, with revelations to the Uninformed of the morals ingeniously concealed by the painters. The Uninformed were also encouraged to debate and to produce papers on literary and political matters, while still unencumbered with the smallest knowledge thereof: for the Enlargement of the Undersanding and the Embellishment of the Intellect. (Morrison, 1896)

Those who attended, Morrison notes, were chiefly

tradesmen's sons, small shopkeepers and their families, and neat clerks, with here and there a smart young artisan of one of the especially respectable trades.

The level of hostility shown by many authors of the time to these people's efforts to acquire some education is curious. One suspects that it was largely due to fear of the consequences of encouraging debate and papers on 'political matters' among the people, whose rise to power was becoming apparent. The spread of democracy had intensified in the Third Reform Act of 1884, which completed male enfranchisement. It also removed the remaining pocket boroughs which had left disproportionate power in the hands of the conservative and country gentry-dominated establishment; it recognised the decisive shift in class structure that the Industrial Revolution had given to Britain. As late as 1942, a historian who grew to manhood under Queen Victoria was still writing, unself-consciously, that

> literature and journalism have been to a large extent debased since 1870, because they now cater for millions of half-educated and quarter-educated people, whose forbears, not being able to read at all, were not patrons of newspapers or books. The small highly educated class no longer sets the standards. . . . (Trevelyan, 1942)

English writers expressed their unease at the possible implications of these trends by sneering at the 'Uninformed'. It was left to an American observer – Henry James – to offer a more complex reaction in his description of a political working men's club, held in a public house:

> There were nights when a blast of imbecility seemed to blow over the place and one felt ashamed to be associated with so much crude fatuity and flat-faced vanity. Then everyone, with two or three exceptions, made an ass of himself, thumping the table and repeating over some inane phrase which appeared for the hour to constitute the whole furniture of his mind. There were men who kept saying 'Them was my words in the month of February last, and what I say I stick to – what I say I stick to' and others who perpetually inquired of the company 'And what the plague am I to do with seventeen bob – with seventeen bloody bob? What am I do to with them – will ye tell me that?' an interrogation which in truth usually ended by producing a ribald reply.

But,

> When the gathering at the 'Sun and Moon' was at its best . . . its temper seemed really an earnest of what was the basis of all its calculations – that the people was only a sleeping lion, already breathing shorter and beginning to stiffen its claws. . . . (James, 1886)

James did not much care for the lion, but at least he acknowledged that it was there, rather than hoping that if sufficiently sneered at it would dematerialise with an embarrassed grin.

His sleeping lion was, however, a purely male one. Indeed, it was a male world, The eight daughters of Lady Fawn were as nothing to her, compared with her son:

> Of all her children he was the least worthy; but he was more important to her than all her daughters.

She believes that special privilege belongs to him, not primarily because he is a peer and Under-Secretary of State but because he is

> the head and only man belonging to the Fawn family. Such a one, when, moved by familial duty, he condescend to come once a week to his mother's house, is entitled to say whatever he pleases, and should on no account be contradicted by anyone.

Her admiration for the male world is not limited to Lord Fawn; she is prepared to excuse Frank Graystock jilting her governess, Lucy Morris, with the reflection that men often behave very badly.

> And at the bottom of her heart she almost thought that they might be excused for doing so. According to her view of things, a man out in the world had so many things to think of, and was so very important, that he could hardly be expected to act at all times with truth and sincerity. (Trollope, 1873)

Trollope clearly feels that Lady Fawn is unfair, and he – together with many other Victorian writers, both male and female – thought that women in general had a poorer life than men. In the 1890s, Gissing allows the Milvain girls to protest quite explicitly against favouritism towards males. The girls live with their mother. Much

of her small annuity goes to support their would-be writer brother;
the girls teach and hate it, but 'don't earn enough for their own
support'. Maud tries to stop her mother from giving Jasper more
money.

> 'We are sacrificed to him as we always have been. Why should
> we be pinching and stinting to keep him in idleness? . . . At this
> rate he will never earn his own living. Who hasn't seen or heard
> of such men? If we had another hundred a year, I would say
> nothing. But we can't live on what he leaves us, and I'm not
> going to let you try.'

Mrs Milvain continues to argue Jasper's case.

> 'Well, all I can say is,' exclaimed the girl impatiently, 'it's very
> lucky for him that he's got a mother who willingly sacrifices her
> daughters to him.' (Gissing, 1891)

Novelists wrote of the unhappiness of many women, and their
testimony is given in later chapters. They were also willing to suggest that particular discriminations – against 'fallen women', for
example, or the provisions of divorce law – were unjustified. But
they were notably unwilling to support more fundamental reforms
to the position of women, or even to describe those few women
who were achieving a tertiary education or training. There are no
impassioned pleas for women's franchise, and the very few 'strong-
minded' advocates who appear are dreary caricatures like Trollope's
Miss Dr Olivia Q. Fleabody (1878) or Henry James's earnest and
tedious Miss Henrietta Stackpole (1881). Women's wrongs achieved
sympathetic coverage; Women's Rights got short shrift.

The problems of women seem to have been viewed as insoluble.
If unmarried, there was always the hope that marriage might prove,
or might have proved, the answer to a maiden's cries. For married
women, there was no prescription but resignation: resignation to
another of those Natural Laws.

> 'It comes to this. Nature doesn't intend a married woman to be
> anything *but* a married woman. In the natural state of things, she
> must either be the slave of husband and children, or defy her
> duty. She can have no time to herself, no thoughts for herself. It's
> a hard saying, but who can doubt that it is Nature's law? I should

like to revolt against it, yet I feel revolt to be silly. One might as well revolt against being born a woman instead of a man.' (Gissing, 1894)

Not until the Great War, which precipitated large numbers of previously non-working women into factories and hospitals and eventually won them the vote, was the possibility of a fuller and more independent life for women recognised. But the 'natural law' by which marriage and motherhood ended such a life continued to be generally accepted until after the Second World War, in fact as well as in fiction, with careers in teaching or in the Civil Service, for example, being abruptly truncated when a woman married.

Natural law, in the Victorian era which did so much to examine and identify the principles of nature and of science, was a sturdy buttress to the prevailing view of women's subordination. It upheld the *status quo* and gave it a 'modern' foundation when other cherished beliefs were being undermined or exploded. Such an attitude may have contributed to the popular reluctance to embrace the notions of contraception and smaller families, when so much of the climate of ideas would seem to have been favourable to them.

The decline in belief in the literal truths of the Bible made it possible to pick and choose from among its texts: 'be fruitful and multiply' lost its imperative when the story of Genesis became part of 'the Romance of Scripture'. Even for those who still believed, it was no longer necessary to see God's hand in illness or suffering; bad drains or the organisms revealed by microscope accounted for the one, and the other could be relieved – as Queen Victoria was to discover in childbirth – by chloroform. Confidence in progress, and the scientific developments which fuelled that progress, made technological innovation welcome. The ideology was optimistic and secular; conducive, as many demographers argue, to the beginning of a transition to fertility decline (e.g. Lesthaege and Wilson, 1986). But if the same ideology strengthened the belief that woman's function and purpose in nature was to have and rear children, it may simultaneously have acted as a brake on change.

3

Visions of Childhood

The nineteenth century might almost be called the century of the child. Children – real and fictional – who at earlier periods would have been written about only in passing, suddenly achieve an independent existence; they become individuals.

One reason for this development may have been the greater visibility of children. Population growth meant that there were both increasing numbers of children, and also an increasing proportion of young people in the population as a whole. The age-structure of the community shifted. The population growth rate in England during the second half of the eighteenth century is believed to have increased from 0.7 per cent to 1.1 per cent a year (Wrigley and Schofield, 1981). These rates are low by modern international standards. Rapid reductions in the death rates in the developing countries from the 1950s onwards resulted in population growth of 2, 3 or even – in a few countries – 4 per cent a year. Despite these differences in the magnitude of growth, one basic result of population growth was evident in Britain then as in Africa today: there were more children.

Not only were there more children around, but more of them were also around their families for a longer period. For the vast majority of people, childhood in any real sense had traditionally consisted of the comparatively brief space of time before the child began to be useful in the home or on the farm. At the very latest, childhood ended when the child started going to work full-time, often at around the age of 12.

As the number of factories expanded during the nineteenth century, childhood initially became, paradoxically, both shorter and longer. Shorter, because the child might begin to be a significant wage-earner at an even younger age than in the past; longer, because the family would keep a contributing child at home for as many years as they could. Describing the Lancashire cotton weavers, Abram (1868) noted

The strength of children is very early utilised in this province. Too brief is the period of immunity from manual toil enjoyed by the operative's child. Let us suppose that our selected urchin is permitted to disport in the street, or frolic upon the hill-slopes with his fellows, during the absence of both of his parents at the mill, until the age of eight; then he is sent to the factory, and enrolled as a 'short-timer'. The next five years are rife with trials. For several hours in the morning he works behind the loom, or beneath the 'mule', acquiring the handicraft which is to bring him bread. In the afternoon he is sent, by legal stipulation and at the charge of his employers, to the factory school. . . . At thirteen the boy 'passes the doctor' (i.e. obtains a medical certificate of age), and becomes a full-timer. . . . All manner of tricks are devised to mislead the medical examiner, and the child who chances to be rejected as under-age regards his fellow who has passed as the object of cruel favouritism. It is hardly necessary to say that this singular anxiety to become a full-time labourer is attributable to the constant prompting of avaricious parents, impatient to seize the proceeds of the child's industry. . . .

As the middle classes expanded, childhood lengthened for an increasing proportion of the nation's young, who were expected to spend years being educated. Especially for boys this meant being packed off to schools from which holidays were rare and any real communication with their parents minimal. However, it happened to girls as well: Kate Nickleby is supposed to have been at school in Devonshire in the early years of the nineteenth century, and her fond but silly mother remembers that Kate wrote

such a delightful letter every half year. . . . The girls wrote all the letters themselves, and the writing master touched them up afterwards with a magnifying glass and a silver pen; at least I think they wrote them. . . . but anyway, I know it was a circular which they all copied. . . . (Dickens, 1839)

That letters home were designed primarily to shed credit on the school, rather than as a means of communicating and strengthening family bonds, remained a convention at least until the 1950s. At my own boarding schools, one's weekly letter home was handed, unsealed, to a teacher to be examined for neatness, spelling and content before being either forwarded or returned for a second attempt. Even where a more enlightened approach prevailed, parents were not expected to take much notice of what their children wrote. Kipling was recalling his own schooldays when, in *Stalky and Co*, he depicts two bullies claiming they never really did their victim any harm:

> 'Yah!' Said Beetle. 'They never really bully. . . . Only knock 'em about a little bit. That's what they say. Only kick their souls out of 'em, and then they go and blub in the box-rooms. Shove their heads into the ulsters and blub. Write home three times a day – yes, you brute, I've done that – askin' to be taken away.' (Kipling, 1899)

From the fifteenth century, Continental Europeans had written with disapproval of the British habit of sending children away from home at an early age (Kendall, 1962) but the practice was not entirely confined to England. The military school in France to which Napoleon received a scholarship at the age of nine had a rule that no boy was to leave, except in dire emergency, throughout the whole five to six years course (Frayling, 1972).

Even when the children were small enough to remain at home, however, those of the middle and upper classes had minimal contact with their parents. Edith, the cousin of Margaret Hale (Gaskell, 1855) has a little boy:

> He was the pride and plaything of both father and mother, as long as he was good; but he had a strong will of his own, and as soon as he burst out into one of his stormy passions, Edith would throw herself back in despair and fatigue, and sigh out 'Oh dear, what shall I do with him! Do, Margaret, please ring the bell for Hanley.'

Because of the presence of governesses and servants, parents had only a limited hand in a child's upbringing. They could feel correspondingly free from responsibility if that child turned out badly.

> The Musgroves had had the ill fortune of a very troublesome, hopeless son; and the good fortune to lose him before he reached his twentieth year; that he was sent to sea, because he was stupid and unmanageable on shore; that he had been very little cared for at any time by his family, though quite as much as he deserved;

seldom heard of, and scarcely at all regretted, when the intelligence of his death abroad had worked its way to Upcross.'
(Austen, 1818)

The Musgroves have washed their hands of him by packing him
off to sea several years before he dies at the age of 19 and even as
a child 'he had been very little cared for . . . though quite as much
as he deserved'. Original sin, or innate badness of character, were
clearly the boy's problem alone.

That view was not solely Jane Austen's; indeed, it persisted
through much of the nineteenth century. Henry Handel Richardson,
born in 1870, based her novel *The Fortunes of Richard Mahoney* (1930)
on the story of her parents. In the book, Polly Mahoney takes into
her home the children of her newly-widowed brother, who have
already suffered neglect and are now hated by their father. The
older child, a six-year-old boy, 'a high-spirited, passionate child',
falls into 'deceitful ways . . . the habit of falsehood was gaining on
him'. Although Polly and her husband decide that there is 'no real
depravity' in him,

> she could not but agree with Richard that it would never do for
> the younger child to be corrupted by a bad example.

She therefore returns the unhappy boy to his father.

Besides circumscribing adult responsibility, limited contact and
communication between parent or other relative and child made
for perfunctory relationships. Fanny Price is sent from home as a
child to be brought up by her wealthier aunt; her years at Mansfield
Park mean that when, in her teens, Fanny returns to visit her family,
she meets with little interest.

> Mrs Price was not unkind – but, instead of gaining on her
> affection and confidence, and becoming more and more dear,
> her daughter never met with greater kindness from her, than on
> the first day of her arrival. The instinct of nature was soon satis-
> fied, and Mrs Price's attachment had no other source. Her heart
> and her time were already quite full; she had neither leisure nor
> affection to bestow on Fanny. Her daughters had never meant
> much to her. She was fond of her sons. . . . (Austen, 1814)

That mother, incidentally, has also been largely forgotten by her sisters because the more subtle separation of differing environments had been fatal to 'natural' connections.

> So long divided, and so differently situated, the ties of blood were little more than nothing. . . . (Austen, 1814)

Fanny Price, whose blood-ties have been dissipated by her removal from her original family, is certainly not a daughter in her adopted home.

> Nobody meant to be unkind, but nobody put themselves out of their way to secure her comfort.

She is patronised by her cousins, put upon by her aunts and generally has the equivocal standing of a poor relation. Her aunt's husband, Sir Thomas Bertram, worries about

> 'the distinction proper to be made between the girls as they grow up; how to preserve in the minds of my *daughters* the consciousness of what they are, without making them think too lowly of their cousin; and how, without depressing her system too far, to make her remember that she is not a *Miss Bertram*. I should wish to see them very good friends, and would, on no account, authorise in my girls the smallest degree of arrogance towards their relations; but still they cannot be equals. Their rank, fortune, rights and expectations, will always be different.' (Austen, 1814)

Despite the discrimination shown to Fanny Price by the Bertrams, Jane Austen herself evidently believed that there was indeed kindness in taking Fanny from her home (and, when we have seen the home life of the Price family, we are expected to think so too). In time, Fanny's younger sister Susan is also rescued from the Price household, to universal satisfaction.

In poorer or less scrupulous families, an intruder like young Fanny might simply become their drudge. All the same, such acknowledged relatives often fared better than an illegitimate son or daughter, who had no standing in the family at all. Mrs Jennings in *Sense and Sensibility* is a good-natured creature, and delights in Colonel Brandon's value as a potential husband for one of her young visitors.

'Two thousand a year without debt or drawback – except the little love-child, indeed; aye, I had forgotten her; but she may be 'prenticed out at small cost, and then, what does it signify?' (Austen, 1811)

It turns out that the 'little love-child' is not the Colonel's at all, but that is not the point: a man was doing all one could possibly expect if he took sufficient responsibility for an illegitimate offspring to pay for its upbringing and for a training so that it could become self-supporting. Beyond that, few wanted to be reminded of the child's existence. Harriet Smith, in *Emma* (Austen, 1816) is

> the daughter of a tradesman, rich enough to afford her the comfortable maintenance which had always been hers, and decent enough to have always wished for concealment.

Throughout her youth and adolescence she languishes unacknowledged as a boarder at school, leaving it only once, for a two-month holiday visit to a neighbouring farm. However, when the farmer, Robert Martin, offers to marry her he is at least 'treated liberally' by her father. Others were less inclined to accept their responsibilities. A boy at Dotheboys Hall could represent, for its headmaster Mr Squeers, not just school fees but

> 'a present besides for putting him out to a farmer, or sending him to sea, so that he might never turn up to disgrace his family, supposing him to be a natural boy, as so many of our boys are . . .'. (Dickens, 1839)

Even those children brought up among their own families did not necessarily have strong family ties, especially once they became economically independent. Jacob Brattle, the miller in Trollope's *Vicar of Bullhampton* (1870), has a son, the 21-year-old Sam, who is immune to, and even rebellious against, family direction.

> Sam had long been deaf to the voices of the women of his family, and, when his father's anger would be hot against him, he would simply go, and live where and how none of them knew. Among such men and women as the Brattles, parental authority must needs lie much lighter than it does with those who are wont to give much and receive much. What obedience does the lad owe

who at eighteen goes forth and earns his own bread? What is it to him that he has not yet reached man's estate? He has to do a man's work, and the price of it is his own, in his hands, when he has earned it. There is no curse upon the poor heavier than that which comes from the early breach of duty between fathers and their sons, and mothers and their daughters.

Duty – the word Trollope uses – seems to have been the main pressure put upon children by their parents, in the absence of closer bonds. It was defined as absolute obedience. Discussing the parallels between his workpeople and children, Mr Thornton in *North and South* (Gaskell, 1855) comments:

'In our infancy we require a wise despotism to govern us. Indeed, long past infancy, children and young people are the happiest under the unfailing laws of a discreet, firm authority.'

Mr Hale, the gentle ex-Vicar, has only a small caveat to make in return, about the need to relax despotism when the child is

in that troublesome stage which intervenes between childhood and manhood:

'Now, the error which many parents commit in the treatment of the individual at this time is, insisting on the same unreasoning obedience as when all he had to do in the way of duty was, to obey the simple laws of "Come when you're called," and "Do as you're bid!" But a wise parent humours the desire for independent action, so as to become the friend and adviser when his absolute rule shall cease.'

A parent's shortcomings were no excuse for a child to refuse to submit to absolute rule: the obedience was expected to be 'unreasoning'. In Rolf Boldrewood's great bushranging story, *Robbery Under Arms* (1888) young Dick Marston grows up in the Australian bush, the son of a surly and embittered ex-convict. Dick's father is described as regularly knocking his wife and children about, and on one occasion when the teenage Dick and his mother have been hit to the ground, the boy comments:

'I think if I'd been another year or so older I'd have struck back – I felt that savage about poor mother I could have gone at him myself – but we had been too long used to do everything he told us; and somehow, even if a chap's father's a bad one, he don't seem like other men to him.'

Samuel Butler had an acutely unhappy childhood; so unhappy that his fictional description of it in *Ernest Pontifex or The Way of All Flesh* (1903) was vividly unforgettable. Indeed, it became for later generations of readers the ultimate comment on the horrors of a mid-Victorian upbringing. 'Is there', Butler asked rhetorically,

any decrepitude so awful as childhood in a happy united God-fearing family?

He described this 'happy united Godfearing family' as one in which the children were the property of their parents, to be abused and victimised and used as outlets for their parents' thwarted passions. Mr Pontifex is 'the violent type of father' who beats his children at the slightest excuse and with ceremonial sadistic pleasure; his wife manipulates their love and emotion with destructive zeal. Both parents justify their behaviour with hypocritical cant; neither has any real interest in the welfare or the development of their unfortunate offspring. They demand duty and obedience from their children, in the kind of way an arbitrary despot might expect it of a serf; affection, or even reciprocal obligations, are beside the point.

Butler's view of the relationships between parents and children was probably an extreme one. We need not assume that every child of the period – or even the majority of children – suffered as poor Ernest Pontifex does. A contrasting and charming portrayal of family relationships is given by Wilkie Collins, in *No Name* (1862), where the teenaged Magdalen dances noisily into breakfast,

taking Mr Vanstone as boisterously round the neck, as if he belonged to some larger order of Newfoundland dog, and was made to be romped with at his daughter's convenience.

Magdalen has a friend, who is no more respectful of her parents; indeed, she has usurped all parental power.

Miss Marrable was that hardest of all born tyrants – an only child. She had never granted a constitutional privilege to her oppressed father and mother, since the time when she cut her first tooth.

But the idea of fathers as tyrannical and violent despots, demanding absolute obedience, is not Butler's alone. Ford Madox Ford (born 1873) had a grandmother who gave him his first conviction

> of great sin, a deep criminality. . . . Similarly my father, who was a man of strong rectitude and with strong ideas of discipline. Yet for a man of his date he must have been quite mild in his treatment of children. In his bringing-up, such was the attitude of parents towards children that it was the duty of himself and his brothers and sisters at the end of each meal to kneel down and kiss the hands of their father and mother as a token of thanks for the nourishment. (Ford, 1911)

The sense that the primary obligation of children to their parents was duty seems to have been a very strong one. It was another of those 'natural laws'. At the same time, it was considered 'natural' that parents should love their children – so long as those children were dutiful – and that children invariably loved their parents, without condition. That view is gently questioned by Mr Charles Cheeryble, in *Nicholas Nickleby*; even natural feelings, he suggested, need regular cultivation if they are to survive.

> Parents who never showed their love complain of want of natural affection in their children; children who never showed their duty complain of want of natural feeling in their parents.

Despite his recognition that 'natural' feelings may shrivel without sustenance, he still sees a child's duty as a prerequisite for parental love. All the same, Mr Cheeryble was hinting at important questions, which others were increasingly debating. The questions turned on the issue of what 'natural' meant, and what it implied for parenting.

The traditional belief that children were a kind of young animal, to be schooled into adult good behaviour by strict discipline, was giving way to two contrasting viewpoints. The first was that each soul – however young – trembled upon the brink of damnation and could only be saved by personal, unremitting, effort. This tenet had long been held by some of the more extreme sects.

James Gillray, born in 1756, was sent to the Moravian Brethren's school. There the children held their own prayer meetings, where they had the liberty to sing and pray, and it was enquired of each how they individually stood with their Saviour. . . . Four centuries of persecution had encouraged a view of death as a glorious release from earthly bondage. At the threshold of understanding, four-year-olds were pushed to terrifying heights of introspection. They welcomed the thought of death, were delighted by funerals and desired passionately not to recover from illnesses. (Hill, 1965)

Gillray's older brother, dying at the school, was visited there by both his parents. His mother heard him affirm that

'he would rather go to our Saviour than go home with her if he was even sure he soo'd thereby recover his health.'

In the nineteenth century, the spread of religious fundamentalism brought the doctrine into the Established Church as well. The sanctimonious Mr Brocklehurst, founder of Lowood School, offers Jane Eyre a tract at their first meeting:

'Little girl, here is a book entitled the Child's Guide; read it with prayer, especially that part containing "an account of the awfully sudden death of Martha G—, a naughty child addicted to false-hood and deceit".' (Brontë, Charlotte, 1847)

To the Rev. Carus Wilson, real-life original of Mr Brocklehurst, children were as – or more – likely to be wicked as good; only perpetual exhortation and threats could keep them on the path of virtue. The series of monthly magazines he published was obsessed with death and damnation. The naughty child is damned, as in the case of the boy who skates on thin ice, and is drowned.

'he left his school. He took his play on the Sunday. And he thought he should go to hell for this. I fear he would go there. How sad it is to think of!' (Gerin, 1967).

So far as children were innocent, Carus Wilson believed, the best thing that could happen to them was to die before they could fall into sin: they would thus provide excellent role-models for their peers. An 11-year-old girl at his Cowan Bridge school became ill, and was asked if she should like to die.

She answered 'Not yet'. 'Why?' 'I should wish to have time to repent, and be a better child.'

Mr Wilson's final comment upon her death was:

'I bless God that he has taken from us the child of whose salvation we have the best hope and may her death be the means of rousing many of her schoolfellows to seek the Lord while he may be found.' (Gerin, ibid.)

The gentle Cornish schoolmistress in Kingsley's *Two Years Ago* (1857) teaches in a Church school, although she is a chapelgoer; the parish is apparently willing to go along with her approach to children, which was

to make them as happy as she could in a world where there was nothing but temptation, and disappointment, and misery: to make them 'fit for Heaven' and then to pray that they might go thither as speedily as possible, this had been her work now for nearly seven years; and that Manichaeism which has driven harder and darker natures to destroy young children, that they might go straight to bliss, took in her the form of outpourings of gratitude (when the first natural tears had dried), as often as one of her little lambs was 'delivered out of the miseries of this sinful world'.

A contrasting but also prevalent view of the child's relationship with God in the mid-nineteenth century was that children were innocent and untouched by the wickedness of the world. This view, based originally on Rousseau's espousal of the purity of nature and the natural man, was taken up with enthusiasm by, among others, Wordsworth.

> ... The Child is father of the Man:
> And I could wish my days to be
> Bound each to each by natural piety.
> (Wordsworth, 1807)

Still more explicitly, in the poem entitled, significantly, 'Intimations of Immortality from Recollections of Early Childhood' (1807) he wrote,

> Not in entire forgetfulness
> And not in utter nakedness,
> But trailing clouds of glory do we come
> From God, who is our home:
> Heaven lies about us in our infancy!

Rousseau's educational prescriptions, based on the assumption of the innate goodness of children, had been expounded in his book *Emile* (1762). Its influence is apparent in the *Notes on Education* written by Caroline Southwood Hill, an admired educational theorist of the 1820s and 1830s.

> Life begins in happiness and this instructs us how we ought to endeavour that it should continue. . . . A child should be placed in circumstances where it can neither do harm nor suffer harm; then it should be left to its own devices. (Bell, 1942)

It was an approach which Dr Thorne (Trollope, 1858) also espoused, although more moderately. He

> had a great theory as to the happiness of children; and though he was not disposed altogether to throw over the precepts of Solomon – always bargaining that he should, under no circumstances, be himself the executioner – he argued that the principal duty which a parent owed to a child was to make him happy. Not only was the man to be made happy – the future man, if that might be possible – but the existing boy was to be treated with equal favour; and his happiness, so said the doctor, was of much easier attainment. . . . 'What!' said his sensible enemies, 'is Johnny not to be taught to read because he does not like it?' 'Johnny must read by all means,' the doctor would answer, 'but is it necessary that he should not like it? If the preceptor have it in him, may not Johnny learn, not only to read, but to like to learn to read?' . . .
> And so the argument went on, neither party convincing the other. But, in the meantime, the children of the neighbourhood became very fond of Dr Thorne.

Others were much more extreme, with their sentimental vision of children as 'little angels'. Jane Eyre (Brontë, Charlotte, 1847), having given a detached assessment of the nature and abilities of her little charge Adela, adds drily:

'This, par parenthese, will be thought cool language by persons who entertain solemn doctrines about the angelic nature of children, and the duty of those charged with their education to conceive for them an idolatrous devotion. But I am not writing to flatter parental egotism, to echo cant, or prop up humbug . . .'.

Jane has already described her young cousins with no 'idolatrous devotion' – John, greedy, violent and a bully; Eliza, headstrong and selfish; Georgiana, bad-tempered and spiteful. It is evident that Charlotte Brontë thought children – especially spoiled children – far from angelic; her sister Anne, drawing on her own experiences as a governess in the novel *Agnes Grey* (1847) gave savage portraits of the tormentors of poor Agnes. Tom Bloomfield is a sadistic thug; his sister Mary Ann is, if anything, worse. However, Anne Brontë did not see their behaviour as sin leading to eternal damnation, but as something which 'a few sound boxes on the ear' might have cured: the children are simply spoiled by doting parents.

Such practical realism warred with the angelic vision in Kingsley, who exhibits a curious contortionism when describing the school-children of his Cornish fishing village. He claims that the school-mistress has fewer sensibilities, and less need to be protected from knowledge of the squalid side of life, than a young lady, because she has already been exposed to the vile. She works in a poor school and with children 'who are in daily contact with coarse sins'. Only a couple of pages later, however, Lord Scoutbush sits down with those same children:

'Now, are you all good children? I'm sure you look so!' said he, looking round into the bright pure faces, fresh from heaven, and feeling himself the nearer heaven as he did so.

Another character comments, seemingly with the author's support,

'Is he not making friends with angels who always behold our Father's face?' (Kingsley, 1857)

All the same, the concept of children as fresh from Heaven re-inforced the alternative concept of children as unregenerate in redrawing the place of children in contemporary minds. A child, whether accountable to God for its salvation, or coming fresh from Him, was not just a junior and dutifully undemanding family

member, but a unique being. Depending on one's religious views
and personal temperament, this unique being might be envisaged
as an innocent not yet contaminated by the world, or brimming
with original sin which only a life of unwearying effort might
counterbalance.

As such, it was infinitely more interesting, and visible, than children had previously been. A child's perceptions of the world, and
the environment which surrounded that child and influenced its
development and character, acquired a new significance.

Novelists seized upon this new development with enthusiasm; it
enabled them to produce fuller and rounder character studies, by
giving a new context to their heroes and heroines. The novel – itself
a growth industry with the expanding potential audience of those
who were able, and had leisure, to read – had found a new lode to
mine.

And mine it they did. Fanny Price in *Mansfield Park* (Austen, 1814);
Oliver Twist and David Copperfield as well as Pip in *Great Expectations* (Dickens, 1838; 1850 and 1861); Jane Eyre (Brontë, Charlotte 1847); Maggy Tulliver in *The Mill on the Floss* (Eliot, 1860); Molly
Gibson in *Wives and Daughters* (Gaskell, 1866): these are just a few
examples of characters whose childhood is described at length and
is central to the book's development.

Concentration on the influences which affected a child also put
new responsibility upon the child's parents. If a child was 'naturally' good, then only a bad upbringing would ruin it. If it were
'naturally' wicked, then the parent must constantly strive to overcome those evil tendencies. *Laissez-faire*, as a doctrine for child
development, was out. Even family relationships had to be worked
at.

Here was a new role for the women of the expanded middle
classes. Few could afford the governesses, or the numbers of servants, that the upper middle class employed to care for their children: the responsibility devolved upon wives and mothers. It rapidly
became their major task. By the 1890s, Nancy Tarrant, who wants
'to be *doing* something', is told by her husband that she has 'a positive
duty' to keep out of the world and concentrate on her child:

> 'You have given the world a new inhabitant, and you are shaping
> it into a man.'
> Nancy laughed, and reflected, and returned to her discontent.
> 'Oh, every woman can do that.'

'Not one woman in a thousand can bear an able-bodied child; and not one in fifty thousand can bring up rightly the child she has borne.' (Gissing, 1894)

Nancy slaves over her baby, and wonders how poor people manage.

'Here am I with one baby, and the constant help of two people; yet he tires me out. Not a troublesome baby, either. . . . Yet the thought and anxiety and downright hard labour for a good twelve hours out of the twenty four! I feel that a second child would be too much for me.'
. . . 'Poor mothers,' said Mary, 'can't give the same care to their children that you give to baby. The little ones grow up, or they don't grow up – that's what it comes to.' (Gissing, ibid.)

Rearing a child properly had now become so challenging and significant that only the finest and most dedicated mothers could hope to be successful. Other women must have felt, with Nancy, that the achievement would be impossible if there were large numbers of children.

The pressure was intensified because not only a child's upbringing, but also its love, became conditional on how a parent behaved. John Dickens, son of a butler, became a clerk in the Navy Pay Office on the recommendation of his parents' former employer. Extravagance and pretensions to gentility brought him to debtor's prison, but just before that final disaster, he had an offer of employment for his son Charles, aged 12. Charles went to work in a bootblacking factory, at six shillings a week for a twelve-hour day sticking labels on the pots.

For the rest of his life, Charles Dickens kept the experience secret. The shame and bitterness he experienced were threaded into many of his books; his parents were never forgiven.

It is wonderful to me, he said, how I could have been so easily cast away at such an age. It is wonderful to me that . . . no one had compassion enough on me – a child of singular abilities, quick, eager, delicate, and soon hurt, bodily or mentally – to suggest that something might have been spared, as certainly it might have been, to place me at any common school. . . . My mother and father were quite satisfied. They could hardly have been more so, if I had been twenty years of age, distinguished at a grammar-school, and going to Cambridge. (Hibbert, 1967)

It is unlikely that his socially-aspirant parents were 'quite satisfied': rather, they were desperate. But the interesting thing about this passage is that Dickens feels quite entitled to judge his father and mother, and to resent what he saw as callous ill-treatment.

He was not alone. Once novels and biographies began to focus on the childhood years, writers became increasingly determined to call their own parents retrospectively to account. A few examples include Samuel Butler's devastating attack in *Ernest Pontifex* (1903); Trollope's *Autobiography* (1883) which devotes considerable space to his unhappy childhood and the way in which he was neglected by his parents; Kipling's *The Light That Failed* (1890) and *Baa Baa Black Sheep* (1907); and Saki (H. H. Munro) in *Sredni Vashtar* (1911).

To the general complaints of tyranny or neglect, Kipling and Saki added another: banishment from their parents. In stories which are among the most frightening of any depictions of childhood, these two, both children of the Empire, recall their despair.

The ties between children and parents had been painfully challenged for more and more families as the British Empire grew. In many of the countries where British administrators, soldiers and others served, the risks of death for a child were much increased compared with Britain. Those who survived early childhood were sent back to England at around the age of six, to live with relatives or be boarded out. The mother of Punch, in *Baa Baa Black Sheep*, prays a slightly illogical prayer at losing her children.

summarised it ran: 'Let strangers love my children and be as good to them as I should be, but let me preserve their love and their confidence for ever and ever.'

Five years later, she visits England to find that the brutalised Punch has lost all sense of his mother, or of love.

He had known that Mamma was coming. There was a chance, then, of another beating. Thank Heaven, Papa wasn't coming too. Aunty Rosa had said of late that he ought to be beaten by a man.

When his mother comes to say goodnight,

he flung up his right arm. It wasn't fair to come and hit him in the dark. Even Aunty Rosa had never tried that. . . . 'Oh, my son – my little, little son! It was my fault – my fault, darling – and yet how could we help it? Forgive me, Punch.' The voice died out in a broken whisper, and two hot tears fell on Black Sheep's forehead.

She can only ask for forgiveness, and hope to rebuild a relationship which, as Kipling makes plain, will never be quite the same again.

Kipling was here writing as an adult, for other adults. But, during the latter part of the nineteenth century, a whole new literature had appeared designed specifically for the children whose existence now loomed so large. Instead of crude moral warnings, children could enjoy books like *Alice in Wonderland* (Carroll, 1865), *Tom Brown's Schooldays* (Hughes, 1857) or even Kipling himself: *The Jungle Book* appeared in 1894.

However, the horrible tracts which Mr Brocklehurst had offered Jane Eyre must have remained a popular genre at least until the 1870s, when Hilaire Belloc as a child encountered them. He was later to produce delightful satires for a generation of adults who could also recall the originals. His parodies immortalised, among others, Matilda, who 'told Lies, and was Burned to Death'; Lord Lundy, 'Who was too freely moved to Tears, and thereby Ruined his Political Career'; as well as Henry King, who 'Chewed Bits of String, and was early cut off in Dreadful Agonies':

> The Chief Defect of Henry King
> Was chewing little bits of String.
> At last he swallowed some which tied
> Itself in ugly Knots inside.
> Physicians of the Utmost Fame
> Were called at once, but when they came
> They answered, as they took their Fees
> 'There is no Cure for this Disease.
> Henry will very soon be dead.'
> His Parents stood about his Bed
> Lamenting his Untimely Death,
> When Henry, with his Latest Breath,
> Cried 'Oh, my Friends, be warned by me,
> That Breakfast, Dinner, Lunch and Tea
> Are all the Human Frame requires. . . .'

With that, the Wretched Child expires.
(Belloc, 1907)

Awful warnings were, however, giving way to an entire new
field of children's literature in which the story, characterisation and
writing, rather than the piety, were preeminent. Even at the lowest
and most mass-produced level such stories had to offer more than
a moral. Jasper Milvain (Gissing, 1891) suggests that his poverty-
stricken sisters should exploit the emerging market for child's story-
books now required for the new generation of children receiving
free schooling, but warns them,

> 'Mustn't be too goody-goody; that kind of thing is falling out of
> date.'

The new children's literature could even admit, to children
themselves, the shortcomings of parents. Mary, in *The Secret Garden*
(Burnett, 1911), is another child of Empire; one young enough to
still be in India with her parents. She gains little from this physical
closeness: her mother, the author bluntly informs a child audience,
never wanted Mary and the nurse is instructed to keep her out of
the way. Mary is a horrid child – sullen, unloving and entirely self-
centred. When her mother dies of cholera, the child is unperturbed:

> as she knew very little of her she could scarcely be expected to
> love her or miss her very much when she was gone.

Her temporary guardians comment on how unattractive she is:

> 'Perhaps if her mother had carried her pretty face and her pretty
> manners oftener into the nursery Mary might have learned some
> pretty ways too. It is very sad, now the poor beautiful thing is
> gone, to remember that many people never even knew she had
> a child at all.'
> 'I believe she scarcely ever looked at her,' sighed Mrs Crawford.

By the end of the nineteenth century, the concept of children
owning a 'natural' duty to their parents seems to have almost
vanished, together with the assumption that love between the generations was automatic and perpetual. If many parents remained
tyrants, they ruled less by an appeal to a moral order than by naked
use of strength.

So much and so nearly complete power was in those elder hands. Of the trivialities or fatalities of Life our cousins and aunts accepted so much and really managed it with admirable smoothness and dignity.

Pain they endured and accepted.

Endless Chaperonage.

Supervision of their correspondence.

The fact that Mother Knew Best.

That Father Says No.

That there is no more to be said on the subject, they accepted. (M. J. Farrell, 1937)

The show of strength hid increasing doubts – doubts about whether the parents have done or will do the right things for their children. By the 1920s, such doubts about one's ability to be a successful parent are quite explicit. In *The Silver Spoon*, Michael Mont, wealthy Member of Parliament of good family, is nevertheless uneasy about his role as father. As his baby son Kit sleeps,

Michael watched him, musing. This manikin, born with all he could possibly wish for within his reach – how were they to bring him up? Were they fit to bring him up, they who had been born – like all their generation in the richer classes – emancipated, to parents properly broken-in to worship the fetish – Liberty? . . . With veneration killed, and self-denial 'off', with atavism buried, sentiment derided, and the future in the air . . . . Without faith was one fit to be a parent? (Galsworthy, 1929)

As the responsibilities of parenting increased during the Victorian era, so too did the costs. Some of those costs were economic. More children attended school, and for longer periods. Whole new industries grew up offering toys and other consumer goods for children, who also began to wear special child fashion clothes instead of being dressed as miniature versions of their parents. It became customary for all except the poorest families to go on an annual holiday, to the country or the seaside.

Other costs were less tangible, but at least as demanding. Good parenting implied spending time with the children, and not just on those annual holidays. Trevelyan (1942) pointed out that among the children's books which became so popular from the 1850s onward, many were designed to be read by parent and child together.

Children's books of which the pleasure was intended to be shared with grown-ups was a characteristic invention of the time.

After a day's work, Mr Darling in *Peter Pan* (Barrie, 1904) comes home to romp with Wendy, John and Michael. Mrs Darling, of course, made a full-time career out of motherhood.

In the short term, some of those middle-class married women who found their role enhanced by the new prestige and responsibility attached to mothering might have been quite content with a traditional family size. The role offered most scope when a child was small: once it vanished into the world of school her significance was much reduced. Only where there were further little ones could her skills and influence be fully used to prove that she was the 'one mother in fifty thousand' who could bring children up properly.

However, if this was indeed one of the factors which may have delayed the transition to lower fertility, it could not for long withstand the alternative pressures which good parenting was putting on couples. The time, effort and financial burden – to say nothing of love – demanded of both parents, as children moved to the centre of the family stage, called increasingly for its concentration on fewer children.

4

Literacy and Learning

An explosion in the numbers of children, as we have already noted, was the first and most obvious manifestation of the rapid growth of population in Britain from the beginning of the nineteenth century. Today, a growth in the number of children in a country produces concern about whether the government will be able to provide an education for them; at that time, such an idea would have seemed absurd to most people. The bulk of the people were not expected to be able to read or write. At best, the daughters of the Squire or Vicar might run a Sunday-school for the village children, largely to supplement – through the learning of a few simple texts from the Bible – the 'moral precepts' which they were expected to pick up from their parents.

Even the children of tradesmen would only become sufficiently literate to be able to figure out their work and simple accounts. In Cornwall in the first decade of the nineteenth century, William Lovett, whose father had died, was taught to read by his great-grandmother, and later

> sent to a boy's school to learn 'to write and cypher', thought at that time to be all the education required for poor people.

He made little progress there, and was eventually transferred to another, where

> I learned to write tolerably well, and to know a little of arithmetic and the catechism, and this formed the extent of my scholastic requirements. (Lovett, 1876)

The rest of a child's education came through apprenticeship of one kind or another. Girls learned to cook and keep house from their mothers; boys began their trade with their fathers. Around the age of 12, both boys and, very often, girls went off to work and upgrade their skills in another household, where they might stay until marriage. Boys were often apprenticed for four or more years, if the parents could afford to pay the master.

Meanwhile, the sons and daughters of the wealthy were tutored or sent off to schools which varied extraordinarily in size and standard. Boys probably did better, on the whole but, even for privileged boys, schooling was haphazard. George Gordon Byron, whose parents might have been aristocratic but whose childhood, in the 1790s, was that of a poor relation, was sent first to

> a mixed and noisy school in a grimy, warehouse-like room, poorly lighted, with a low ceiling and dusty floor. . . . Byron wrote: 'I learned little there, except to repeat by rote the first lesson of Monosyllables – "God made man, let us love him" – by hearing it often repeated, without acquiring a letter.' (Marchand, 1971)

Becoming heir-presumptive to the Byron title, he was transferred to the Aberdeen Grammar school, where

> the only branch of study was Latin, taught in the traditional manner that made lessons a deadly chore. . . . Writing was an 'extra', which he studied at Mr Duncan's writing school (Marchand, ibid.).

Subsequently, Harrow and the boredom of Greek translations proved to be little better:

> The drilled dull lesson, forced down word by word,
> In my repugnant youth (quoted in Marchand, op. cit.)

At least Byron learned something, however dull his tuition. At the smaller private schools in the first half of the nineteenth century, sycophancy seems to have been the main lesson. Dickens, who repeatedly attacked such schools in his novels, remembered his own experience of the Wellington House Academy with sharp distaste:

> I don't like the sort of school to which I once went myself, the respected proprietor of which was by far the most ignorant man I have ever had the pleasure to know. . . . whose business it was to make as much out of us and to put as little into us as possible . . . the abject appearance and degraded condition of the teachers . . . I have never lost my ancient suspicion touching that curious coincidence that the boy with four brothers to come always got

the prizes. In fact, and in short, I do not like that sort of school, which is a pernicious and abominable humbug. (Hibbert, 1967)

In the same spirit, Miss Pinkerton in *Vanity Fair* (Thackeray, 1847) is outraged when her sister suggests giving the usual school-leaving present of a dictionary to Becky Sharp as well as to Amelia Sedley.

Miss Sedley's papa was a merchant in London, and a man of some wealth; whereas Miss Sharp was an articled pupil, for whom Miss Sedley had done, as she thought, quite enough. . . .

But some children suffered from worse than humbugs. The purpose of a school was not necessarily to educate; some existed simply to keep – or lose – unwanted children at a convenient distance from family or guardians. The infamous Bowes Academy in Yorkshire, which was one of the models for Dotheboys Hall in *Nicholas Nickleby* (Dickens, 1839), had become the subject of a lawsuit brought by the parents of two of its unfortunate inmates. The boys had been so neglected and ill-fed as to have gone blind; in evidence it came out that ten other children had also gone blind while at the school. Between 1810 and 1835 twenty-five schoolboys had been buried in the local churchyard. As the boys were frequently beaten, ate food crawling with maggots, and slept five to a bed, this was hardly remarkable. More unexpected is the fact that although the proprietor of the school was found guilty, and forced to pay damages, he remained in charge and the school continued to do business (Hibbert, 1967).

Girls were seen to need even less learning than their brothers. 'Be good, sweet maid, and let who will be clever' was the prevailing theme. The basic type of school for a middle-class girl in the first half of the nineteenth century was probably something like the one in *Emma* (Austen, 1816)

Mrs Goddard was the mistress of a school – not of a seminary, or an establishment, or anything which professed, in long sentences of refined nonsense, to combine liberal acquirements with elegant morality, upon new principles and new systems – and where young ladies for enormous pay might be screwed out of health and into vanity – but a real, honest, old-fashioned Boarding-school, where a reasonable quantity of accomplishments were sold at a reasonable price, and where girls might be sent to be out of the way and to scramble themselves into a little education, without any danger of coming back a prodigy.

The 'accomplishments' which the girls acquired at Mrs Goddard's were probably much the same as those offered at Miss Pinkerton's academy for young ladies, although the latter's charges undoubtedly reflected the more pretentious title of her establishment. Miss Pinkerton's final report on Amelia Sedley states:

> 'In music, in dancing, in orthography, in every variety of embroidery and needlework, she will have been found to have realised her friends' fondest wishes. In geography there is still much to be desired; and a careful and undeviating use of the blackboard, for four hours daily during the next three years, is recommended as necessary to the acquirement of that dignified deportment and carriage, so requisite for every young lady of fashion.' (Thackeray, 1847)

An almost identical catalogue of accomplishments was being paraded across the channel by Emma Roualt (Flaubert, 1857) who

> had been brought up at an Ursuline convent and been what is called 'well educated'; in consequence of which she was expert at dancing, geography, drawing, fancy needlework and the piano. It was too much!

Jane Eyre's education at Lowood, the charitable school designed to produce young women who could earn their livings as teachers or governesses, was about the best available at the time. Jane became

> qualified to teach the usual branches of a good English education, together with French, Drawing and Music. In those days, reader, this now narrow catalogue of accomplishments would have been held tolerably comprehensive

adds the narrator (Brontë, Charlotte, 1847).

The 'usual branches of a good English education' would have included those on Miss Pinkerton's list, together with Bible study and some English grammar. Certainly, those minimum accomplishments over-qualified Jane for becoming a teacher in a small village school, as her anxious cousin points out:

'It is a village school: your scholars will be only poor girls – cottagers' children – at the best, farmers' daughters. Knitting, sewing, reading, writing, ciphering, will be all you have to teach. . . .' (Brontë, Charlotte, 1847)

The village where young Tom Brown (Hughes, 1857) was brought up was 'blessed, among other things, with a well-endowed school' for the local children. Young Tom, who of course had a governess, would go down to the village after his lessons were over, and hang around the school to wait for his friends. When the schoolmaster complained to Squire Brown that his son distracted the boys and was a nuisance, it was agreed,

> Tom was not to go near the school till three o'clock, and only then if he had done his own lessons well, in which case he was to be the bearer of a note to the master from Squire Brown; and the master agreed in such case to release ten or twelve of the best boys an hour before the time of breaking up, to go off and play in the close.

That the school should provide playmates for the Squire's son rather than an education for its pupils seems to have been taken for granted.

Given the indifferent level of schooling, and the fact that educational qualifications, in any formal sense, were not a prerequisite either for university entrance or for a career, it is perhaps not surprising that even the rising middle classes were ambivalent about its value at first. The wealthy manufacturers of Milton [Manchester] described by Mrs Gaskell (1855) did not send their sons for higher education, or even allow them to finish their schooling.

> They were mostly at the age when many boys would still be at school, but, according to the prevalent, and apparently well-founded notions of Milton, to make a lad into a good tradesman he must be caught young, and acclimatised to the life of the mill, or office, or warehouse. If he were sent to even the Scotch Universities, he came back unsettled for commercial pursuits; how much more so if he went to Oxford or Cambridge where he could not be entered till he was eighteen? So most of the manufacturers placed their sons in suckling situations at fourteen or fifteen years of age, unsparingly cutting away all off-shoots in the direction of literature or high mental cultivation, in hopes of throwing the whole strength and vigour of the plant into commerce.

The Manchester manufacturers were not alone in fearing that education might subvert the young. Mr Burton, of the great engineering firm of Burton and Beilby, had immediate doubts about taking Harry Clavering as an articled pupil, because Harry had been to university and become a teacher. Finding the young man fussy about selecting his lodgings, Mr Burton

> in his own mind formed the idea that this new beginner might have been a more auspicious pupil, had he not already become a fellow of a college. (Trollope, 1867)

He soon takes the opportunity to tell Harry about the success of his sons:

> 'But they began early, Mr Clavering; and worked hard – very hard indeed.'

An old sea-captain in *The Return of the Native* (Hardy, 1878) is convinced education of any kind is subversive:

> 'Ah, there's too much of that sending to school in these days! It only does harm. Every gatepost and barn's door you come to is sure to have some bad word or other chalked upon it by the young rascals: a woman can hardly pass for shame, some times. If they'd never been taught how to write they wouldn't have been able to scribble such villainy. Their fathers couldn't do it, and the country was all the better for it.'

The idea of graffiti as the net result of education was probably idiosyncratic. Other parents had more practical objections. The 1851 Census report noted that

> it is evident that even the lowest amount of wages which the child of a labouring man will receive (from 1s 6d to 2s per week) must be of so great a relief to the parents as to render it almost hopeless that they can withstand the inducement, and retain the child at school in the face of this temptation. (Mann, 1851)

This opportunity cost of schooling was far more important, he claimed, than the question of whether or not the parents had to pay for schooling.

It is not for the sake of *saving a penny* per week that the child is transferred from the school to the factory, but for the sake of *gaining a shilling or eighteenpence* per week.

The child of a factory worker could make a significant financial contribution to the family. While a rural child of a similar age was unlikely to be able to do that, it was nevertheless beginning to be useful; its parents too might be unsure about the gains from education. Typical, perhaps, was the reaction of a New Forest cottager describing her young daughter Susan's enrolment in the parochial school:

'... I miss her sadly. I used to teach her what little I knew at nights. It was not much to be sure. But she were getting such a handy girl, that I miss her sore. But she's a deal above me in learning now.' And the mother sighed. (Gaskell, 1855)

Despite losing Susan's services around the house, and a feeling that her daughter was growing away from her because of her more sophisticated knowledge, Susan's mother had continued to send her to school: she must have felt that in some mysterious way Susan was going to need more education than had been traditionally provided to people like her. It is a feeling that Mrs Gaskell's Mr Bell, an elderly and very conservative Cambridge Fellow, does not initially share. Even the limited curriculum of the parochial school is, he asserts, more than Susan requires:

'I'm all wrong,' growled Mr Bell. 'Don't mind what I say. I'm a hundred years behind the world. But I should say, that the child was getting a better and simpler, and more natural education stopping at home, and helping her mother, and learning to read a chapter in the New Testament every night by her side, than from all the schooling under the sun.' (Gaskell, ibid.)

Susan's mother, though, goes on to describe a quarrel she has had with her neighbour, Betty Barnes. Betty has stolen her cat, and boiled or roasted it alive, so that its cries will compel the powers of darkness to fulfil her wishes – which, in this instance, are to get back her husband's Sunday clothes, tricked from her by a gypsy. Susan's mother is quite convinced that the charm works, but is angry 'that her cat had been chosen out from all others for a sacrifice'.

Nothing that her visitors can say alters her belief in this country superstition:

> at the end, the bewildered woman simply repeated her first assertion, namely, that 'it were very cruel for sure, and she should not like to do it; but that there were nothing like it for giving a person what they wished for; she had heard it all her life; but it were very cruel for all that'. Margaret gave it up in despair, and walked away sick at heart.
> 'You are a good girl not to triumph over me,' said Mr Bell.
> 'How? What do you mean?'
> 'I own, I am wrong about schooling. Anything rather than have that child brought up in such practical paganism.' (Gaskell, op. cit.)

This curious vignette provides, I think, a clue to one of the ways in which even a very basic educational process might have influenced people's lives. Superstitions – attempts to change or avert the mysterious workings of fate – were widespread until at least the middle of the nineteenth century. Eustacia, daughter of the old sea-captain who believed that education's sole output was graffiti, is suspected of ill-wishing the ailing child of a villager. As a result, she is first stabbed with a stocking-needle in church 'to put an end to the bewitching' and later, when the child continues to decline, its mother makes a wax image of Eustacia, fills it with pins and then melts it in the fire.

> It was a practice well known on Egdon at that date, [1840–50] and one that is not quite extinct at the present time. (Hardy, 1878)

Even the most humble parish schools opened the possibility of influences beyond those of the immediate family circle. Indeed, that is partly what Susan's mother has recognised when she sighs at her daughter being far above her in learning. The undermining of superstition – whether through the incredulous laughter of a Vicar's or Squire's daughter, or the determined assault of a self-educated Rationalist – was, quite possibly, an unforeseen outcome of exposure to schooling.

Despite the reservations of many people, demand for formal schooling was increasing, fuelled, on the one hand, by the rising numbers of children as the population expanded and, on the other, by the concerns both of individuals and society. As the Industrial Revolution gathered momentum and more and more families were sucked into cities and factories, it became apparent that children were no longer receiving the moral and practical instruction from their homes or other sources which had been their traditional providers of education. Indeed, the reports of various committees and commissions into the conditions of work of children and young people show the children interviewed as not merely illiterate, but brutalised and ignorant to the utmost extent. They were unaware of what England was, or who Queen Victoria might be; they confused Jesus and the Devil; sometimes they were unable even to add up the coins in their meagre wage-packets. That many were like this, we must believe: the reports are depressingly consistent all the way down to General William Booth's famous attack, *In Darkest England* (1890).

But we should also remember that these children, interviewed by intimidating government officials whose purposes were a mystery to them, were probably bewildered and frightened, and that they were being asked questions which the officials thought they should know the answer to, rather than ones which related directly to their lives. Many must have had more initiative, and natural intelligence than appears in the record, simply to have survived. Dropped suddenly into the savage world of an industrial slum, one wonders how well those educated officials would have fared. Disraeli, although those same parliamentary reports were his source material for *Sybil* (1845), presents his adolescent industrial workers – Devilsdust and his cronies – as shrewd, quick-tongued and streetwise; so too does Dickens.

The reasons why so many young people grew up without many basic skills were obvious. In 1839, almost half of all factory operatives were under the age of 18. Among both adults and child-workers, more than half were female. Dr Hawkins, Commissioner for Lancashire in the Factories' Inquiry Commission, pointed out (Engels, 1845) that girls

> have neither the means, time, or opportunity to learn the ordinary duties of household life; but if they had them all, they would find no time in married life for the performance of these duties. The mother is more than twelve hours away from her child daily, the baby is cared for by a young girl or an old woman, to whom it is given to nurse. Besides this, the dwelling of the

mill-hands is too often no home but a cellar, which contains no cooking or washing utensils, no sewing or mending materials, nothing which makes life agreeable and civilised, or the domestic hearth attractive.

Pressure to provide some basic education came not only from philanthropists like Lord Shaftesbury, but from a variety of other sources. Active churchmen were shocked that so many children were growing up as heathen. The growing numbers of nonconformists resented the established Church-based education of the Sunday-schools and the exclusion of their children from them: they called for alternative State-funded systems to be available to all.

More importantly, perhaps, the industrial society needed not just unskilled or semi-skilled labourers but overseers, foremen, clerks, technicians and draughtsmen; a host of literate white-collar workers. One such was Octavia Hill, who in 1852 at the age of 14 was running a cooperative toy factory.

She had to take stock from time to time and show a balance sheet . . . She learnt to keep accounts with meticulous accuracy, and to be methodical and punctual in all her work. 'I have often thought of your accounts which would not balance,' she wrote to Mary Harrison, 'and thought what a terrible state I should be in if mine would not, as I have eight or ten different accounts to keep' (Bell, 1942).

The first significant state intervention towards meeting these various needs came with the Factory Act of 1834, which applied only to textile mills, and limited work to a nine-hour day for children between the ages of 9 and 13. Compulsory school attendance for two hours a day was prescribed for those children, whose pay was to be docked by a penny a week to pay for the teachers.

Engels (1845) commented that school attendance, as specified in the 1834 Factory Act, remained wholly a dead letter:

The manufacturers employed as teachers worn-out old operatives, to whom they sent the children two hours daily, thus complying with the letter of the law; but the children learned nothing.

It is difficult to believe that even with better teaching a 9-year-old could have picked up much after working for nine hours in a factory. Schools outside the factories were no more satisfactory. Engels also quoted a Birmingham inquiry which reported one teacher, when asked if she gave 'moral instruction', saying that she did not: at threepence a week it was too much to ask. Other teachers, according to the inquiry, did not understand the question.

A major problem, not only with the factory or village schools, was the shortage of adequate teachers. Expanding demand inevitably outstripped supply, and the skills even of those who were considered suitable teachers were minimal. In Staffordshire, where only half the children attended a Sunday-school even occasionally, the teachers were smiths or miners, who frequently could not read, and who wrote their names with difficulty. Even 'educated' teachers, however, were the products of Miss Pinkerton's and Mrs Goddard's establishments, with a very limited list of accomplishments to pass on.

The Prettyman sisters, who keep a well-thought-of school in Silverbridge in the 1860s, have added a few items – notably Roman history – to the typical curriculum of the early part of the century. But they are not much better informed than were earlier generations of women, as emerges when Miss Anne brings her sister news that the magistrates have bound over a local clergyman, Mr Crawley, for trial because he cannot explain his possession of a cheque.

'They have found him guilty; they have indeed. They have convicted him – or whatever it is, because he couldn't say where he got it.'

You do not mean that they have sent him to prison?'

'No – not to prison; not as yet, that is. I don't understand it altogether, but he's to be tried again at the assizes. In the meantime he's to be out on bail ...'.

... Miss Anne Prettyman was supposed to be especially efficient in teaching Roman history to her pupils, although she was so manifestly ignorant of the course of the law in the country where she lived.

'Committed him,' said Miss Prettyman, correcting her sister with scorn. 'They have not convicted him. Had they convicted him, there could be no question of bail.'

'I don't know how all that is, Annabella, but at any rate Major Grantly is to be the bailsman, and there is to be another trial at Barchester.'

'There cannot be more than one trial in a criminal case,' said Miss Prettyman, 'unless the jury should disagree, or something

of that kind. I suppose he has been committed, and that the trial
will take place at the assizes.'

'Exactly – that's just it.' Had Lord Lufton appeared as lictor,
and had Thompson carried the fasces, Miss Anne would have
known more about it. (Trollope, 1867)

Kingsley (1857) too was unimpressed with the spread of girls'
boarding schools which he saw as producing bewildered little fools
like the doctor's daughter in a Cornish fishing town. He described
her, and others like her, as

> less educated than the children of their parents' workmen,
> sedentary, luxurious, full of petty vanity, gossip and intrigue,
> without work, without purpose, except that of getting married
> to anyone who will ask them. ...

He recommended, instead of these private genteel establishments,
something like the high-school system of America.

Most people, however, were less concerned with the content of
schooling than the prospects it opened up – prospects of greater job
security, enhanced status and even a change in class. This could
affect the whole family as well as the individual; as we shall see in
a later chapter, having a teacher in the family, for example, meant
that other siblings might refuse manual work as demeaning.

A doctor like Charles Bovary would not have been likely to marry
the daughter of a struggling small farmer – 'if it hadn't been for the
cabbage crop last year, the poor fellow'd have a job to keep his
head above water!' (Flaubert, 1857) – but for Emma's convent education. She had distanced herself from the farm; indeed she was no
longer either capable of or willing to undertake farm work.

If an education helped to expand the middle classes, the children
of those new classes were, should they receive the liberal education
of the gentry, well on the way to being recognised as being gentle
themselves. Among the boys, a liberal education increasingly meant
going to a public school and university. The public schools, under
the influence of reforming headmasters like the famous Dr Arnold
of Rugby (1828–42), underwent a great boom between the 1840s
and 1860s.

Again, the standards of education which they offered seem to
have been of less importance than their social significance. A Royal
Commission in the early 1860s was quite critical of the achievements

of the expanded public schools, saying that they were less concerned with the quality of their teaching, or the appropriateness of the subjects they taught, than with providing 'the education of a gentleman'. In practice this continued to mean – as it had in Byron's time – classical literature, to which the influence of people like Arnold had added character-formation and exercise.

The strictures of the Royal Commission were irrelevant to the parents of prospective schoolboys, who were not sufficiently impressed by education to care whether it was up-to-date or not. *Tom Brown's Schooldays* helped to spread the fame of Dr Arnold and Rugby, and the father of its hero probably stands for many of the fathers who sent their boys there or to similar public schools. Squire Brown, sending Tom off to Rugby for the first time, debates what advice to give the boy.

'Shall I tell him to mind his work, and say he's sent to school to make himself a good scholar? Well, but he isn't sent to school for that – at any rate, not for that mainly. I don't care a straw for Greek particles, or the digamma; no more does his mother. What is he sent to school for? Well, partly because he wanted so to go. If he'll only turn out a brave, helpful, truth-telling Englishman, and a gentleman, and a Christian, that's all I want,' thought the Squire. (Hughes, 1857)

From a public school a boy would, increasingly, expect to go to university. Oxford and Cambridge, to which admissions had remained relatively steady between the 1820s and 1860, suddenly found themselves having to cater to these new expectations: Cambridge doubled its intake of students by 1880 (Kitson Clark, 1962). But the universities, with their continuing emphasis on classical studies, were designed to complete the education of a gentleman, rather than to offer qualifications for a career.

The younger sons of the gentry had traditionally confined themselves to the Church, the law or the armed services. New careers were now becoming available to those with a living to earn, but their status was, all too often, doubtful. Doctors – whether surgeons, physicians or apothecaries – had an ambiguous respectability; there were others, such as engineers, in a similar position – or lack of position. Confronted with the upwards pressure of an ambitious and newly-educated lower middle class, they decided to protect and enhance their status through the creation of professional bodies which required particular standards of education or training. The mid-nineteenth century saw the establishment of professional status for architects in 1834–35; mechanical engineers in 1847; solicitors in a series of Acts over the period; while the Medical Act of 1858 regulated surgeons, physicians and apothecaries.

Developments like these made educational qualifications increasingly important, and fuelled the demands for a national educational system. State funding was first introduced in 1870. For the children of the poor, schooling became virtually universal, except in particularly deprived areas. As late as 1896 Morrison could write of his East End slum, the Jago:

> There was a Board School ... where children might go free, and where some few Jago children did go now and again, when boots were to be given away, or when tickets were to be had, for tea, or soup, or the like. But most parents were of Josh Perrott's opinion: that school-going was a practice best never begun; for then the child was never heard of, and there was no chance of inquiries or such trouble. Not that any inquiries were common in the Jago, or led to anything.

Schooling was in any case not necessarily productive. In the East Anglian village which Ronald Blythe called 'Akenfield' (1969) the old farm labourer Len Thompson remembers his schooling in the 1880s:

> 'The school was useless. The farmers came and took boys away from it when they felt like it, the parson raided it for servants. The teacher was a respectable woman who did her best. Sometimes she would bring The Daily Graphic down and show us the news.'

One recalls Squire Brown's cavalier attitude to the village children's schooling, forty years earlier. The inspector's reports for the period confirm the school's inadequacy.

> It is true that 5 standards and an infants' class, with only one Monitress as an assistant, constitute an arduous task, but it is difficult to believe that the results need have been so poor....

We have already met another Akenfield villager, old John Grout, who went to work on the railways as a young man, and who recalled that among his fellow railwaymen several could not write.

Laurie Lee (1959) fared a little better:

> Our village school was poor and crowded. . . . We learned nothing abstract or tenuous there – just simple patterns of facts and letters, portable tricks of calculation, no more than was needed to measure a shed, write out a bill, read a swine disease warning. Through the dead hours of the morning, through the long afternoons, we chanted away at our tables. Passers by could hear our rising voices in our bottled-up room on the bank: 'Twelve-inches-one-foot. Three-feet-make-a-yard. Fourteen-pounds-make-a-stone. Eight-stone-a-hundred-weight.' We absorbed these figures as primal truths declared by some ultimate power. Unhearing, unquestioning, we rocked to our chanting, hammering the gold nails home. 'Twice-two-are-four. One-God-is-love. One-Lord-is-King. One-King-is-George. One-George-is-Fifth.' So it was always; had been, would be for ever; we asked no questions; we didn't hear what we said; yet neither did we ever forget it.

None of this suggests that most children during the nineteenth century received much of an education, or that the schooling they did get would have been particularly effective in teaching them logical thought, or reasoning. Certainly it was not designed to encourage them to question established customs or traditions, or even to express some sort of individuality.

And yet, from 1871 onwards, young couples did begin to behave in one fundamentally different way to couples of the past, by beginning to have smaller families. Some of these couples would have been the first generation of their kin to acquire any education, however inadequate: others would have been, by then, the sons and daughters of parents who had themselves participated in the educational revolution which changed Britain from a predominantly illiterate to a literate country within a century. And it is generally thought that the spread of education must have influenced those couples in their family building – as it seems to today in the Third World, where any sort of schooling is associated with smaller family size.

Some of the ways in which education may have affected people have already been hinted at. Mrs Gaskell's little Susan would, Mr

Bell suggested, discard her traditional superstitions as the result of her schooling; Hardy's comment on their dwindling role in village life as the century progressed seems to confirm that Mr Bell was right.

Susan is interesting for another reason, though: her mother misses her sorely, because she was beginning to be useful about the house. One demographic theory (Caldwell, 1976) argues that people begin to want fewer children when those children, instead of being a net benefit to the household through their work, become a cost. Going to school not only prevents them from being useful in the home, but involves sending them off tidily dressed and shod, as well as the buying of books and other equipment.

There is no doubt, too, that the spread of education during the nineteenth century both facilitated and fuelled what other demographers have called 'the rising aspirations with regard to intergenerational mobility' (Lesthaege and Wilson, 1986). Education could – and did, as we have seen – propel people into a different class, but the fundamental distinction was between the literate and the illiterate. Once a person could read and write, the possibility of more education (and greater status) for his or her child became a feasible ambition.

Education beyond the village school needed even greater parental investment, and one which could seldom be managed if a couple had a large family. Emma Bovary's father somehow managed to pay for her convent schooling, but then she was an only child. That in itself is not entirely surprising (though it would have been even less surprising had she been a boy) since family size in France had been falling since the 1820s.

Another feature of the growth in literacy in the nineteenth century was that much of it took place in the towns and cities. The Industrial Revolution had swept together vast numbers of men and women from all over the country and landed them, as R. H. Tawney (1920) said, 'without tradition or organisation, in towns which were little better than mining camps'. Churches were few and, even if there were a conscientious Vicar there was nothing much he could do with his vast number of new unruly 'parishioners'. The old rural social hierarchy of landowners and tenants, of squires and gentry, was entirely absent. In such a climate, radical ideas could grow and flourish. What was more, where people could read, such ideas could spread at a great speed.

Higgins, the Trade Unionist weaver of Mrs Gaskell's Milton, thinks of going to the country when he is blacklisted by the manufacturers after a strike. Margaret Hale knows he will never stand it:

'You would not bear the dulness of the life; you don't know what it is; it would eat you away like rust. Those that have lived there all their lives, are used to soaking in the stagnant waters. They labour on, from day to day, in the great solitude of steaming fields – never speaking or lifting up their poor, bent, downcast heads. The hard spadework robs their brain of life; the sameness of their toil deadens their imagination; they don't care to meet to talk over thoughts and speculations, even of the weakest, wildest kind, after their work is done; they go home, brutally tired, poor creatures! caring for nothing but food and rest. You could not stir them up into any companionship, which you get in a town as plentiful as the air you breathe, whether it be good or bad – and that I don't know; but I do know that you, of all men, are not one to bear a life among such labourers. What would be peace to them, would be eternal fretting to you. Think no more of it, Nicholas, I beg.' (Gaskell, 1855)

Some of the townsmen had thoughts and speculations which might be wild but were far from weak. The London Working Men's Association was created by, among others, William Lovett, who, despite the lack of schooling described earlier, had become a political activist and leader of the Chartist movement. The LWMA managed to form over 100 similar associations around the country during 1837 alone; its concerns were not only with the People's Charter for reform of the franchise, but with the conditions of workers; with education; with international affairs; with a wide range of social as well as economic issues. In the cities, and in smaller towns as well, working men's study groups spread rapidly and are still commemorated today in the – frequently imposing – buildings which were erected to house the Working Men's Institutes, Literary Institutes and so on.

It was these men who agitated for the removal of duty on newspapers, so that the poor could read them. Duty on newsprint was reduced from fourpence to one penny in 1835 and abolished in 1855. Of the reduction, Lovett (1876) commented that

To. . . . the subsequent cheap newspapers that resulted from our warfare, may also be traced the great extension of the coffee-rooms

and reading-rooms of our large towns, and the mental and moral
improvement resulting from their establishment.

Lovett's claims would have been disputed by many: we saw in
Chapter 2 how poorly such efforts at self-improvement were
regarded by other writers. Nevertheless, those who acquired snip-
pets of contemporary thought, and even the readers of scandal
sheets and cheap romances, discovered through them that there were
other people, other views and other worlds besides their own. Those
whose energy and ambition and curiosity were greater could learn
to challenge established authority on anything from the structure
and functions of Parliament to the nature – and even very existence
– of God.

5

The Single Girl

Adolescence, as an in-between time bridging childhood and becoming an adult, was a concept unknown in the nineteenth century. Most children went to work full-time at around the period they entered their teens. Those who became agricultural workers often started at an even earlier age, and as late as 1851 Horace Mann said, in the Census Report, that all children from the age of 9 upwards were

> considered capable of certain kinds of agricultural labour. Indeed, some persons qualified to judge are of opinion that the business of a farm labourer cannot be thoroughly acquired if work be not commenced before eleven or twelve.

Most of these very young children would have remained at home, at least for a few years. If the parents were involved in some sort of cottage industry, the child would be increasingly active in the work, and his or her earnings were unlikely to be distinguished from the contributions of other family members.

By the time they were 14 or thereabouts, they would be entitled to a full, adult wage, and often they moved from the family home at the same time. There seems to be little evidence that they routinely sent some of their wages home; instead they saved what they could towards an eventual marriage.

The growth of industry only intensified the tradition of a short childhood. The Census Report continued,

> In mechanical employments labour begins at an even earlier age. Children begin to be employed in needle making, in button making, as errand boys and in various other capacities, some as early as six, others at any time from 6 to 10. (Mann, 1851)

We saw, in earlier chapters, that Octavia Hill started work at 13; a year later she was in charge of the toy-furniture factory, where in addition to keeping all the accounts it

75

was Olivia's duty to choose the shape and colour of each piece of toy furniture, to assign the various processes to each child, to price the finished article, to see each suite of furniture neatly packed and sent over to the show room, and finally to pay each child for the amount of work she had accomplished. (Bell, 1942)

Even among the middle classes, at 15 Isobel in *Cousin Henry* (Trollope, 1879) is keeping house for an elderly relative.

Factory children were at least as likely as their rural equivalents to move out of the parental home at an early age. Thus young Devilsdust in *Sybil* (Disraeli, 1845) lives on his own and his girlfriend Harriet, who had been helping to support her family

long murmured at her hard lot; working like a slave, and not for herself. And she has gone, as they all go, to keep house for herself.

The biggest change in this centuries-old pattern during the nineteenth century was that increasingly the young people's work was done in factories, rather than in domestic service or agriculture. The extent of the shift should not be overemphasised. In 1851 almost a third of girls and women in England and Wales were in paid employment, according to the Census. By far the greatest number – almost a million – were in domestic service; the textile industries accounted for under half a million women. However, domestic service was to become increasingly less popular as alternative employment opportunities extended. An article in the *Edinburgh Review* of 1862 pointed out some of the reasons.

The liberty which endears factory life to both lads and lasses is in strong contrast with the restraints of domestic service. . . . The annual or half-yearly festival – the picnic in summer and the ball in winter – which is a conspicuous event in factory life, excites a vast sensation throughout the neighbourhood, and is an occasion of great pride or vanity to the members. Servant girls and footboys see the vans go by in the summer morning, and hear the fiddles and dancing in the winter evening, and feel they are 'in bondage' and 'get no pleasure'. They cannot dress as the factory lads and lasses do – buying and wearing whatever they take a fancy to. Worse still, they do not have the daily stimulus and amusement of society of their own order. Beyond their kitchen mates, they seldom have any free and prolonged conversation; while the day-workers pass to and from the factory in groups, and can take walks, or spend the evenings together. The maid-servant must have 'no followers', while the factory girl can flirt to any extent. Servant girls rarely marry, while factory girls probably always may, whether they do or not. . . .

It was true, the article continues, that factory workers might have less security, and 'the burden of temptation is fearfully heavy' – but despite this public opinion was against domestic service. 'In one word, it is independence against dependence.'

Disraeli's Harriet works in a factory, in the usual squalid conditions of those days. Nevertheless, when she leaves home she goes to share 'a very nice room in Arbour Court, No. 7, high up; it's very airy.' From her airy room, Harriet can stroll the lively streets of Mowbray in the evenings, exchange back-chat with young men, lie about in bed until noon on her day off, and be taken out for the evening to the 'Temple of the Muses', a kind of gin palace of such splendour that Harriet says, 'It's just as I thought the Queen lived in.'

Further up the social scale, the range of employment opportunities narrowed considerably. A 'lady' without any skills to offer could become a 'companion'. Miss Macnulty (Trollope, 1874) is a classic example. She

was as utterly destitute of possessions or means of existence as any unfortunate, well-born middle-aged woman in London. To live upon her friends, such as they might be, was the only mode of life within her reach. It was not that she had chosen such dependence; nor, indeed, had she endeavoured to reject it. It had come to her as a matter of course,– either that or the poor-house. As to earning her bread, except by that attendance which a poor friend gives,– the idea of any possibility that way had never entered her head. She could do nothing,– except dress like a lady at the smallest possible cost, and endeavour to be obliging.

Companions like Miss Macnulty had to run errands and play cards or read or otherwise attempt to amuse their employers, and above all provide a receptive and sycophantic audience. Poor Miss

Macnulty, 'who was an honest woman in her way' found this part of her work the most difficult, and was frequently abused as a result.

> Upon the whole, however, to be called a fool was less objectionable to Miss Macnulty than were demands for sympathy which she did not know how to give.

She cannot even be successful as a parasite.

Miss Macnulty was middle-aged, but young women became companions too. The redoubtable Miss Stanbury in *He Knew He Was Right* (Trollope, 1869) takes one of her nieces, Dorothy, to live with her, explaining to Dorothy's mother,

> 'Should you agree to this, she will be welcome to receive you or her sister . . . in my house any Wednesday morning between half past nine and half past twelve. I . . . will make her an allowance of £25 per annum for her clothes as long as she remains with me. I shall expect her to be regular at meals, to be constant in going to church, and not to read modern novels.'

Dorothy was lucky; if living with a relative, a companion did not necessarily receive any kind of fixed wage – Lady Linlithgow only gives her cousin Miss Macnulty occasional presents of money. However, only well-established and comfortably-off families provided the possibility of shelter for a destitute relation. The newly-rich, like the Mayor of Casterbridge (Hardy, 1886), have no useful connections, so when his daughter becomes unhappy at home after her mother's death she has to get a job as a paid companion to a stranger.

A young woman from the middle classes who had received a better education than was needed by a companion could become a governess. She would only do this if her family were poor, or had died without leaving her an income. To be a governess was in no sense a desirable career. Although it was somewhat higher in prestige than being a servant, it was otherwise not very different.

A governess was expected to conform to the views and requirements of the household where she was employed. More significantly, becoming a governess often closed the door on any possibilities of a brighter future: a governess, like a domestic servant, was not allowed 'followers'. When Frank Greystock, in

The Eustace Diamonds (Trollope, 1874) begins to show an interest in
Lucy Morris, his mother warns him to be careful:

> 'Remember her position,' said Mrs Dean to her son.
> 'Her position! Well;– and what is her position, mother?'
> 'You know what I mean, Frank. She is as sweet a girl as ever
> lived, and a perfect lady. But with a governess, unless you mean
> to marry her, you should be more careful than with another girl,
> because you may do her a world of mischief.'
> 'I don't see that at all.'
> 'If Lady Fawn knew that she had an admirer, Lady Fawn would
> not let her come into her house.'

Lady Fawn, in fact, is an extremely kind employer, who generally treats Lucy as one of the family. If one compares Lucy's
experiences with those of an earlier fictional governess, Agnes
Grey (Brontë, Anne, 1847) it is clear that Lady Fawn was an absolute paragon.

In her first post, Agnes Grey suffers from uncontrolled little fiends
with doting parents; in her second from arrogant young women
who are encouraged to treat her as a kind of servant; in both homes
her status is equivocal, her employers patronise her, and her comfort is unconsidered. In contrast,

> Lady Fawn fully appreciated her treasure, and was, and ever had
> been, conscientiously anxious to make Lucy's life happy. But she
> thought that a governess should not be desirous of marrying, at
> any rate until a somewhat advanced period of life. A governess,
> if she were given to falling in love, could hardly perform her
> duties in life. No doubt, not to be a governess, but a young lady
> free from the embarrassing necessity of earning bread, free to
> have a lover and a husband, would be upon the whole nicer. So
> is it to be born to £10,000 a year than to have to wish for £500.
> Lady Fawn could talk excellent sense on this subject by the hour,
> and always admitted that very much was due to a governess
> who knew her place and did her duty. She was very fond of Lucy
> Morris, and treated her dependant with affectionate considera-
> tion;– but she did not approve of visits from Mr Frank Greystock.
> (Trollope, ibid.)

There were, however, compensations even for a life as a governess. Agnes Grey defines her reasons for wanting to become one:

To go out into the world; to enter upon a new life; to act for myself; to exercise my unused faculties; to try my unknown powers; to earn my own maintenance. . . . (Brontë, Anne, 1847)

Lucy Morris, too, had this sense of independence, and 'a well formed sense of her own identity'.

She was quite resolved to be somebody among her fellow-creatures,– not somebody in the way of marrying a lord or a rich man, or somebody in the way of being a beauty, or somebody as a wit; but somebody as having a purpose and a use in life. She was the humblest little thing in the world in regard to any possible putting of herself forward, or needful putting of herself back; and yet, to herself, nobody was her superior. What she had was her own, whether it was the old grey silk dress which she had bought with the money she had earned, or the wit which nature had given her. (Trollope, op. cit.)

There is a strong echo of Jane Eyre in this passage. Jane also has a strong sense of self-worth – of her individual identity being the equal of anybody else's – which is stressed again and again throughout the novel. She will not be a 'slave' to Rochester even though she loves him; when she is going to be married she feels annoyed and degraded by his attempts to buy her clothes and jewels. Her determination to have only the simplest of clothes is not due to some Puritan dislike of pretty things but to her lack of any money of her own.

'It would, indeed, be a relief', I thought, 'if I had ever so small an independency; I can never bear being dressed like a doll by Mr Rochester, or sitting like a second Danae with the golden shower falling daily around me . . .'. (Brontë, Charlotte, 1847)

Each of these women sees herself as having an intrinsic value and standing which does not simply derive from breeding, income or worldly status. They are not chattels; they can provide for themselves. All the same, when Jane discovers that Mr Rochester is already married, and has run away from Thornfield Hall, she prefers teaching in a humble parish school to becoming a governess again: it would be 'servitude with strangers'.

As the century wore on and schools mushroomed, becoming a

teacher provided an increasing number of women with an alternative – and more attractive – way of earning a living. What a teacher
wore, her time of going to bed, and her choice of breakfast – to take
some everyday details – were her own business.

Teaching not only provided greater independence, but could raise
the status of a whole family. The *Edinburgh Review* (1862) pointed
out that before the spread of better-quality education, most of the
girls who now became pupil-teachers would have gone into domestic service. Today, when there was a pupil-teacher in a family,

> the other members assume that the whole household have risen
> in rank. When once a pupil-teacher becomes a certificated school-
> mistress, her sisters consider it beneath them to be in service.
> When one girl becomes Miss A or B, the others desire to leave off
> their caps, and to take rank among the educated class. If that
> fortunate individual has dined at the house of a school manager,
> and has had a footman stand behind her chair, the rest cannot be
> contented with the kitchen ... they look about for the chance of
> obtaining some post as a teacher of something – of becoming in
> some way, however humble, connected with a school; and if that
> be out of reach, they will follow any employment which exempts
> them from 'bondage' to authority, and enables them to call them-
> selves 'Miss', at whatever risk of precarious subsistence, poverty,
> or even want.

Here, then, was a further contribution to the expansion of the lower
middle class.

Socially and economically better-off women were simply expected
to sit at home and wait for Mr Right to come along. It was, indeed,
a sign of gentility that a girl did not need to earn her own living,
or even to do much housework in her own home. We have already
seen, in Chapter 4, that the spread of education had produced large
increases in the number of women who felt themselves unfitted for
work in the house or elsewhere by being 'educated'; their families
agreed.

This important development was not confined to Britain. In France,
for example, farmer Roualt is much relieved when Charles Bovary
comes along as a suitor for his daughter Emma (Flaubert, 1857).

> Old Roualt would not have been sorry to get rid of his daughter,
> who was of little use to him about the place. He excused her in
> his own mind, as being too clever for farming. ...

Emma's convent education had unfitted her for the toil and drudg-
ery of a poor farmer's world; so far as we are told, her main contribution since returning home has been to do some sketches which
now hang on the farmhouse walls.

But if the daughters sit at home, how can they find an eligible
match? Social pretensions without sufficient economic support could
make it very difficult to meet a suitor. Emma was lucky that Charles
Bovary, being a doctor, made a professional visit to her father,
because the old farmer certainly could not afford to give her a
social life through which she could meet gentlemen.

The Milvain women in *New Grub Street* (Gissing, 1891) are described as having received 'an intellectual training wholly incompatible with the material conditions of their life'. Their father, a
veterinary surgeon, having died, they live with their mother on her
small annuity and are considered to have airs of superiority because they do not mix much in local society. In fact, however, lack
of money for clothes, and other 'simple luxuries', let alone to enable
them to entertain, kept them apart from

> the society which would have welcomed them, for they could not
> bear to receive without offering in return.

For girls like Dora and Maud Milvain, marriage was quite difficult.
Their education had left them disinclined (and probably not well-
equipped) to marry the small shopkeepers or tenant farmers who
otherwise might have been their lot. Lack of means kept them from
mixing with young men further up the social scale.

For other women, it was not so much lack of means which kept
them immured at home, as parental protectiveness. Beatrix Potter,
the daughter of a comfortable middle-class family, describes in her
diary – at the age of 28 – going to visit some cousins in Gloucester-
shire:

> I went to Harescombe on Tuesday the 12th. of June. I used to go
> to my grandmother's, and once I went for a week to Manchester,
> but I had not been away independently for five years. It was an
> event.
>
> It was so much an event in the eyes of my relations that they
> made it appear an undertaking to me, and I began to think I
> would rather not go. I had a sick headache most inopportunely,
> though whether cause or effect I could not say, but it would have

decided the fate of my invitation but for Caroline, who carried me off. (Linder, 1966)

When she hoped to return the hospitality, her parents made excuses to prevent her inviting the cousins. Beatrix wrote forlornly,

I am afraid that it would have resulted in rubs, but I would so very much have liked to have Caroline, and I am afraid they rather expected to be asked. . . .

Among the upper classes, the London Season offered a formalized ritual for introducing young women to young men; but here, more than ever, considerable cost was involved. The Arundell women, growing up in the 1840s, expected to be launched into society in order to make a good marriage. Despite being born into the old Catholic nobility, their father had no particular property and hence had become a wine-merchant. He and his family had divided their time between London and the country, but it now became essential to economise for the girls' coming-out. For a few years the Arundells.

found it expedient to withdraw altogether from London, in order to husband their resources. (Blanch, 1954)

Daughter Isabel was not a good investment: at the end of her 'Season' she had refused every suitor. Before the family could bring her back into circulation, they had to economise even further, by retiring to Boulogne.

The necessity to marry becomes all too clear when one realises what the life of the unmarried stay-at-home daughter was like. Isabel suffered severely in Boulogne

at that time the haunt of impoverished English society, both select and shady. The two sets never met. There were fast streets and respectable promenades. The Arundells moved among the slow set in unimpeachable dullness. . . . Walks along the jetty with Mama. Hateful needlework in the salon, or a covert eying of the fast set, glimpsed shopping. . . . (Blanch, ibid.)

For two years this was her existence; only one intoxicating glimpse of the man she loved instantly, and was eventually to marry – Richard Burton – enlivened the boredom.

Unmarried 'girls', whatever their age, remained locked in this sheltered and deadly routine. When Lady Fawn is told that her son is engaged to Lizzie Eustace, she brings her eldest unmarried daughter Augusta to London to visit her. Unfortunately for Augusta, they call first on Mrs Hittaway, Lady Fawn's married daughter, who says that Lizzie is a quite dreadful person and that the engagement must be broken off. Lady Fawn decides that all the same she must visit Lizzie, as she has promised; she is also, naturally, curious to see the woman,

> but Mrs Hittaway's words had the effect of inducing her to leave Augusta where she was. If there were contamination, why should Augusta be contaminated? Poor Augusta! She had looked forward to the delight of embracing her sister-in-law;– and would not have enjoyed it the less, perhaps, because she had been told that the lady was false, profligate, and a vixen. As, however, her position was that of a girl, she was bound to be obedient,– though over thirty years old,– and she obeyed. (Trollope, 1873)

M. J. Farrell (1937), writing about the life of an upper-class family in Ireland at the end of the century, described this subservience as still continuing.

> 'Is that the gong?'
> 'My dear, do hurry! I suppose I'd better fly down. One of us ought to be in time.'
> 'Oh, do wait, Muriel. If you're late too, it won't matter so much.'
> ... Diana went heavily and as slowly as she dared behind Muriel's fluttering, skipping rush down stairs. They both paused outside the library door and looked at each other like naughty little girls who are late for prayers again. Diana was ashamed of the reality of moments like this. Having been caught by herself and Muriel feeling like a silly little girl, she felt angry and unbalanced and summoning a sort of sulky dignity she walked into the library as boldly as she could. At this time Diana was twenty-eight and Muriel thirty-five years of age. But then neither of them was married or ever likely to achieve that state of bliss or dignity. They had no caste. They were the girls at home.

Margaret Hale, in *North and South* goes, after her parents' death, to live with her frivolous married cousin in London.

The course of Margaret's day was this; a quiet hour or two before a late breakfast; an unpunctual meal, lazily eaten by weary and half-awake people, but yet at which, in all its dragged-out length, she was expected to be present, because, directly afterwards, came a discussion of plans, at which, although they none of them concerned her, she was expected to give her sympathy, if she could not assist with her advice; an endless number of notes to write, which Edith invariably left to her, with many caressing compliments as to her *eloquence du billet*; a little play with Sholto as he returned from his morning's walk; besides the care of the children during the servants' dinner; a drive or callers; and some dinner or morning engagement for her aunt and cousins; which left Margaret free, it is true, but rather wearied with the inactivity of the day. . . . (Gaskell, 1855)

She is not a poor relation; her guardian has insisted on providing her with an income sufficiently large to make her an independent contributor to the household. But her daily round seems to have been little different to that undertaken by a paid 'companion'.

Such an existence of excruciating boredom was – as the century progressed and economic growth added to the numbers who wanted their daughters to be genteel – the lot of an increasing proportion of young women. It was an existence which most of them would have to endure for years, because the Victorian era continued Britain's traditional pattern of very late marriages; two out of every five women in England and Wales, and almost half of the women in Scotland, were still unmarried at ages 25–29 (Teitelbaum, 1984).

Even more depressingly, for many women being 'the girls at home' was a fate which would last a lifetime. In England and Wales in 1851, there were fewer than 91 men aged 25–29 for every 100 women in the same age-group. In Scotland, the imbalance was even worse: there were just under 83 men for every hundred women. Although the actual figures during the remainder of the century fluctuate a bit, very low ratios of men to women continue throughout the period. Heavy levels of male migration – especially to the United Sates and the colonies – were the major cause of the problem; its effects were obvious. Almost one in seven women in England and Wales remained unmarried at ages 45–49; in Scotland more than one in five were unmarried (Teitelbaum, ibid.).

Some women subsided into becoming the family drudge, like Hilary Bonham Carter, in 1844 a close friend of Florence Nightingale, who was 'a victim of family life' (Woodham-Smith, 1951). Discovering her artistic talent, the celebrated Mary Clarke begged Mrs Bonham Carter to allow Hilary to train seriously as a painter.

> But Hilary could not be 'spared'. Now she was spending her life housekeeping, teaching her younger sisters, doing the flowers, and, as a concession, attending a 'ladies atelier' in London, where so little was expected that lessons were taken 'when social engagements permitted'.

Others might go, or be forced, to almost any length in an attempt to avoid remaining single and dependent. Several of Trollope's novels describe young women, whose looks are almost their sole asset, being hawked about the country by relatives determined to sell them to the highest bidder. Examples include Arabella Trefoil in *The American Senator* (1877) as well as Lucinda Roanoke (*The Eustace Diamonds*, 1874). These young women can only dress themselves attractively by the rather squalid strategies of tricking their suppliers; colluding with their creditors by suggesting that the goods are an investment in a future marriage; and by making bets with young men for gloves and other garments.

They have usually become rather hard, but not hard enough to be happy in their lives. Indeed, their most notable characteristic is barely suppressed rage and loathing of men – and of their calculating families. Lucinda Roanoke, the night before her wedding, threatens to kill herself or her prospective husband; her aunt knows that

> the horror the bride expressed . . . was no mock feeling, no pretence at antipathy. She tried to think of it, and to realise what in truth might be the girl's action and ultimate fate when she should find herself in the power of this man whom she so hated. But had not other girls done the same thing, and lived throught it all, and become fat, indifferent, and fond of the world? . . . There was, no doubt, very much of bitterness in the world for such as them,– for persons doomed by the necessities of their position to a continual struggle.

The next morning Lucinda is found in a state of complete nervous collapse. For an hour and a half her aunt tries to persuade her to go on with the wedding, using threats, scolding and weeping.

'Do you want to destroy me?' Mrs Carbuncle said at last.
'You have destroyed me,' said Lucinda. (Trollope, 1874)

She has, indeed, gone mad.

The seeds of destruction were in the system itself, as well as in
poor Lucinda. With a growing proportion of educated women
waiting about for years for a marriage which might never eventuate, they began increasingly to question their role in the world –
and the world itself. For 'the world' could not entirely be kept away
from them, however hard parents might try. Ford Madox Ford (1931)
remembered

> taking the young daughter of my father's most intimate friend,
> who was Queen Victoria's Master of Music, on the River Blythe
> in a canoe. I talked to her about the conditions of the poor. Next
> day her mother Lady Cusins said to me:
> 'Fordie, you are a dear boy. Sir George and I like you very
> much. But I must ask you not to talk to dear Beatrice. . . . about
> Things!'

Keeping 'Things' from the young Beatrices of the period was not
as easy as Lady Cusins thought. Somehow they did hear about
conditions – of the poor, of hospitals and prisons, housing, and
even prostitution. And what they heard often fused with what they
had been taught about their accountability to God. Even the smallest
and most innocent child was going to have to stand up and answer
for itself and be judged. Being a woman who had led a harmless
and sheltered (if deadly dull) existence would not be enough to
save one at the Day of Judgement. Neither would faith. 'For God
shall bring every work into judgement . . .' and these women could
never convince themselves that He would be content with embroi-
dered slippers.

'On February 7th, 1837, God spoke to me and called me to His
service', wrote Florence Nightingale (Woodham-Smith, 1951). She
was only 17 and it was to be several years before she was to know
what kind of service she would be asked to perform. In the meantime, she had to endure years of what her friend Mary Clarke described as 'Faddling twaddling and the endless tweedling of
nosegays in jugs' (Woodham-Smith, ibid.), but she never doubted
that she must do something with her life.

A decade later, for Octavia Hill, helping to keep her family was still not enough. She wrote to her sister,

> 'I wish, oh how I do so long, to do something. . . . Do you think I shall ever be able to do anything really useful?' (Bell, op. cit.)

Both women were extremely unusual; and not solely in their own time and environment. They would, one feels, have been remarkable in any age. But they were not so exceptional in their determination to contribute in some way to the overall good. Isabel Arundell, for example, occupied her frustrated years of waiting for Richard Burton by work among 'fallen women' in London.

Concerns like the ones of these three women are mirrored by those of Margaret Hale. As soon as she inherits a substantial fortune, and is therefore able to confront her cousins with confidence, she makes up her mind to take

> her life into her own hands. . . . She had learnt, in those solemn hours of thought, that she herself must one day answer for her own life, and what she had done with it; and she tried to settle that most difficult problem for woman, how much was to be utterly merged in obedience to authority, and how much might be set apart for freedom in working. . . . She charmed her reluctant aunt into acquiescence with her will. So Margaret gained the acknowledgment of her right to follow her own ideas of duty.
>
> 'Only don't be strong minded,' pleaded Edith. 'Mama wants you to have a footman of your own; and I'm sure you're very welcome, for they're great plagues. Only to please me, darling, don't go and have a strong mind; it's the only thing I ask. Footman or no footman, don't be strong minded.' (Gaskell, op. cit.)

Twenty years later, Dorothea, in *Middlemarch* (Eliot, 1872), is struggling with the same problem.

> She could not reconcile the anxieties of a spiritual life involving eternal consequences, with a keen interest in guimp and artificial protrusions of drapery. Her mind was theoretic, and yearned by its nature after some lofty conception of the world which might frankly include the parish of Tipton and her own rule of conduct there. . . . What could she do, what ought she to do? – she, hardly more than a budding woman, but yet with an active conscience

and a great mental need not to be satisfied by a girlish instruction comparable to the nibblings and judgements of a discursive mouse. With some endowment of stupidity and conceit, she might have thought that a Christian young lady of fortune should find her ideal in life in village charities, patronage of the humbler clergy, the perusal of Female Scriptural Characters, unfolding the private experience of Sara under the Old Dispensation and Dorcas under the new, and the care of her soul over her embroidery in her own boudoir – with a background of prospective marriage. . . .

Dorothea already runs an infant school, which she had introduced in the village, and is busy designing model cottages, which she persuades her admirer and future brother-in-law, Sir James, to build on his estate. When Mr Casaubon appears on the scene and shows an interest in her, Dorothea is overwhelmed by the prospects she sees opening in front of her.

> 'I should learn everything then. . . . It would be my duty to study that I might help him the better in his great works. There would be nothing trivial about our lives. . . . And then I should know what to do, when I got older: I should see how it was possible to lead a grand life here – now – in England.' (Eliot, ibid.)

That Dorothea is making a fatal mistake in her assessment of Mr Casaubon does not detract from her sincerity of purpose, or from George Eliot's obvious sympathy with the views of her character.

Lady Aurora, in *The Princess Casamassima* (James, 1886) is another who combines the need to do something with her life with a despairing recognition of her barren existence and prospects. She works in the slums of Camberwell, because

> 'Already when I was fifteen years old I wanted to sell all I had and give to the poor. And ever since I've wanted to do something: it has seemed as if my heart would break if I shouldn't be able!'

She comes from a family of twelve children of whom eight are daughters; only one is married, 'and we're not at all handsome'. Neither is their father rich; he would not be able to provide a good marriage portion to increase their eligibility. They all spend the autumn and winter in the country,

'... and the rain drips, drips, drips from the trees in the big dull park where my people live ... when one's one of eight daughters and there's very little money (for any of us at least) and nothing to do but to go out with three or four others in mackintoshes, one can easily go off one's head. Of course there's the village, and it's not at all a nice one, and there are the people to look after, and goodness knows they're in want of it; but one must work with the vicarage, and at the vicarage are four more daughters, all old maids, and it's dreary and dreadful and one has too much of it ... I want to live!'

'And do you call this life?'

'I'll tell you what my position is if you want to know: it's the deadness of the grave!'

Behind the demands for training, further education, careers and a vote which were to gather in volume as the century drew to a close lay the guilt, as well as the frustration, of generations of women trapped into despair by a system which was increasingly widespread and at the same time increasingly dysfunctional.

Their dilemma was summed up by Caroline Helstone, in *Shirley*, in four pages of bitter soliloquy. The girls in her neighbourhood

'have no earthly occupation but household work and sewing, no earthly pleasures but an unprofitable visiting, and no hope, in all their life to come, of anything better. . . . The great wish, the sole aim of every one of them is to be married, but the majority will never marry; they will die as they now live. They scheme, they plot, they dress to ensnare husbands. The gentlemen turn them into ridicule; they don't want them; they hold them very cheap. They say – I have heard them say it with sneering laughs many a time – the matrimonial market is overstocked. Fathers say so likewise, and are angry with their daughters when they observe their manoeuvres – they order them to stay at home. What do they expect them to do at home? If you would ask, they would answer, sew and cook. They expect them to do this, and this only, contentedly, regularly, uncomplainingly, all their lives long, as if they had no germs of faculties for anything else – a doctrine as reasonable to hold as it would be that the fathers have no facilities for eating what their daughters cook or for wearing what they sew. Could men live so themselves? Would they not be very weary? And when there came no relief to their weariness, but only reproaches at its slightest manifestations, would not their weariness ferment in time to frenzy? . . .' (Brontë, Charlotte, 1849)

From that frenzy came the demands, increasing as the century wore away, for training and careers, which was ultimately to give to middle-class women the independence which was the one blessing their poorer sisters already had. Independence was to bring, in addition, personal fulfilment and confidence in their claim to equality with men. But, at the end of the Victorian age, few had any hope of achieving it. 'Give them scope and work', Caroline Helstone had demanded. Despite the efforts of a few brave pioneers, most single Victorian women of the middle and upper classes remained trapped in their weariness and desperation.

6
Love and Marriage

The legendary Victorian father, fixing his daughter's suitor with a chilly eye while demanding if the young man could keep her in the style to which she was accustomed, was no joke. To the unfortunate suitor, he was more often an immovable force on which any hopes of matrimony were dashed. For Britain was a part of a unique marriage pattern, which extended across Western Europe. That pattern, quite unlike any other in the world, involved late ages at marriage and substantial numbers of people never marrying at all (Hajnal, 1965). Why the age of marriage in Western Europe was so high is not known, but one of the theories is that it, and the high proportion of people who did not marry at all, were among the ways in which people in Western Europe controlled overall fertility and ensured that those who did marry could support the children they produced.

Even within a single family the age at which marriageable children married depended on their positions within that family. In eighteenth-century Tuscany, for example, Corsini (1977) found that younger children married at older ages than the first born, and that age of marriage, for both men and women, increased depending on whether they were the second, third, or fourth and upwards child. In other words, families found it more difficult with each successive child to get together the resources to launch younger children into marriage.

The level of difficulty depended upon the type of household economy – thus, in Tuscany, the stoneworkers, who gained an independent cash income, married earlier than sharecroppers. Male children of sharecroppers usually remained within the extended family, and the marriage of a son 'would increase the present and future number of "mouths", e.g. the number of consumers in the farm, in a manner more than proportionate to that of the "labour" ' that the new additions to the extended family provided (Corsini, ibid.).

From at least as far back as the sixteenth century, people in Britain have married at quite a late age. During much of that time, the mean age of marriage for women was around 26 years; during the eighteenth century it fell to around 23 years, but even that was high compared to non-Western European countries. During the nineteenth century, the age of marriage rose again, reaching a mean of 25.8 years for women in 1851. It dipped very slightly to 25.2 years in 1871 before increasing to 26 at the end of the century (Wrigley and Schofield, 1983). In Scotland the mean age of marriage was always slightly higher.

These overall average figures hide considerable regional variations. Taking Scotland as an example, the median age at marriage ranged from less than 23 years in West Lothian to more than 26 in the Orkneys and in Bute (Anderson and Morse, 1993). Different social and economic patterns in different regions affected both marriage age and the numbers of children people produced when they did marry. In crofting areas, where access to land was limited, a son might have to wait until he inherited a plot before he married. Other young men left the area to seek their fortunes; yet others remained single. Between a quarter and a third of the women in these areas never married at all. Many women in the Border regions also remained unmarried, but for different reasons: the textile mills provided opportunities for them to earn a living and brought many more females into the area; there were no equivalent jobs for men. As the mill-owners disliked employing married women, loss of an independent income was something of a deterrent to marrying one of the few men around.

Social class – or, rather, occupation – also affected the age at which people married. In Britain in 1886 working-class men married, on average, at 24; tradesmen at 27 and professionals, not until they were above 31 (Rose, 1986). The reason was that couples were generally expected to be able to be self-sufficient: to be able to set up their own household, however rudimentary. Long before the Industrial Revolution offered new employment in new urban centres for young people, it had been the custom for centuries in Britain to send adolescent children away to work – on farms, or as servants or apprentices. It also seems to have been the custom that the young people kept their wages for their own future, rather than remitting them back to the family. Once a couple decided to marry, their joint savings went into setting up a separate household (MacFarlane, 1986). The amount they needed to get married varied according to the social expectations within each class.

An ordinary workman's earnings peaked in the early adult years, so that some might be able to marry at an earlier age than was the norm within their class. The story of 'an average specimen of the respectable farm labourer' (Stratton, 1864) describes him leaving school around the age of 10, and, after a few years' work, leaving home and going into lodgings.

> But he soon is ambitious of all the distinctions of early manhood, and after passing through the half-dozen violent attachments which matrons denominate calf love, he is seen some fine morning, before he is two-and-twenty, on his way from church, with his bride, who is seventeen. . . .

They either lodge with his parents, or take a couple of furnished rooms until they can afford a cottage.

Not very much was needed to set up a working-class home. Samuel Bamford, a weaver, described his as consisting of one room,

> clean and flagged. . . . A humble but cleanly bed, screened by a dark old-fashioned curtain, stands on our left. At the foot of the bed is a window closed from the looks of all street passers. Next are some chairs, and a round table of mahogany; then another chair, and next it a long table, scoured very white. Above that is a looking glass with a picture on each side of the resurrection and ascension on glass, 'copied from Rubens'. A well-stocked shelf of crockery ware is the next object, and in a nook near it are a black oak carved chair or two, with a curious desk, or box, to match; and lastly, above the fire-place, are hung a rusty basket-hilted sword, an old fusee, and a leather cap. (Bamford, 1844)

A tradesman, on the other hand, would probably have undergone an apprenticeship before saving to set up his business. William Lovett was apprenticed for seven years as a ropemaker; finding it difficult to get work, he eventually undertook another apprenticeship as a cabinet-maker. He married, at the age of 26, a lady's maid, having

> provided for this event as far as possible, by making my own furniture, and by otherwise providing for her a comfortable home. (Lovett, 1876)

Professional men very often went to university before embarking on the increasingly stringent qualifications demanded before they could practice; then they had to become established before risking the expense of marriage.

Phineas Finn (Trollope, 1869) takes his law degree at the age of 22 and is then sent (at his father's expense) to a barrister's chambers for a further three years. Once he has been called to the Bar, his father offers to support him for a further three years while he begins to practice in Dublin. When Phineas determines to stand for Parliament instead, he is still dependent on the parental allowance. It is no wonder that all he can say to the girl back home is:

> 'Of all men in the world, I suppose that I am the last that has the right to be in love. I dare say I shall marry some day ... but not until I'm forty or perhaps fifty years old.'

Similarly, Lydgate, the 27-year-old doctor in *Middlemarch* (Eliot, 1872) who has used up almost all of his tiny inheritance in buying a practice in the town, and who has ambitions of making his name in medical research, knows that

> he could not marry yet ... he did not mean to marry for the next five years.

Unfortunately, he does not stick to his resolution, and the expense of setting up a household, together with the extravagance of his wife Rosamond, come close to wrecking his future.

When marriages took place so late among the middle classes, a sensible parent was not going to encourage an early betrothal. In *The Go-Between* (Hartley, 1953) two Edwardian schoolboys discuss engagements.

> 'How long do engagements last?' I asked. Marcus would be sure to know. . . .
> 'In the case of grooms, gardeners, skivvies and such-like scum,' said Marcus, 'it may go on for ever. With people like ourselves it generally doesn't go on very long.'
> 'How long?'
> 'Oh, a month or so. Deux mois, trois mois.'

The risks of a long engagement were particularly acute for a girl. Should she remove herself from the marriage-market, and then find herself abandoned by a fiancé who developed other interests and affections as he matured, her chances of finding another man would be small. For every 100 women aged 25–29 there were, throughout the second half of the nineteenth century, only about 90 men; emigration had removed some of the possible husbands. Given the competition, the older, jilted woman was likely to lose out to a younger competitor.

When Mary Lowther's lover discovers that his father has stolen his inheritance, and that he has nothing but his Army pay (insufficient to support a gently-bred wife) everybody insists that the engagement must be broken off.

The question had come to be discussed widely among their friends, as is the custom with such questions in such circumstances, and Mary had been told from all sides that she was bound to give it up,– that she was bound to give it up for her own sake, and more especially for his; that the engagement, if continued, would never lead to a marriage, and that it would in the meantime be absolutely ruinous for her,– and to him. . . .

Her aunt sums it up:

'. . . such an engagement is destructive to both parties.'
    'For myself,' said Mary, 'it can make no difference.'
    'It will make the greatest difference. It would wear you to pieces with a deferred hope. There is nothing so killing, so terrible, so much to be avoided.' (Trollope, 1870)

However, as Mary's aunt indicated, a long engagement was to be avoided by the gentleman, too. On the one hand, by committing himself too early, he was excluding himself from the possibility of coming across a more eligible prospect as his fortune and status improved. On the other, he might be distracted from his work by desire for the loved one.

An engaged couple was not quite so strictly chaperoned as were other young people, and a long engagement therefore posed additional risks. Parents were well aware of the difficulties of ensuring celibacy among young adults, and that it could be achieved only by relentless social controls. Hence both the cult of purity, and the rigorous supervision to ensure that young people were never left alone together for any length of time. Young men, of course, might 'sow their wild oats' so long as they did so at a safe distance; the enormous number of prostitutes in Victorian Britain catered to their needs and perhaps gave them experience of contraception, while reinforcing popular belief that birth control was used only by the immoral.

Not only virginity, but something more was demanded of a potential bride; she was expected to be 'innocent', free from any thoughts of love or sexuality until after she had received a proposal. What shocked mid-nineteenth century readers about Jane Eyre was that she made no secret of falling in love with Mr Rochester long before his first offer of marriage.

A few decades later, it had become possible gently to mock the shibboleth of purity. Thus Gilbert, in the Savoy opera *Patience*, describing an aesthete carrying a flower in his 'mediaeval hand':

And everyone will say
As you walk your flowery way
'If he's content with a vegetable love which would certainly not suit *me*
Why, what a most particularly pure young man this pure young man must be!' (Gilbert, 1883)

Mrs Brookenham, in the same era, takes advantage of the more liberal atmosphere to carry on her usual sophisticated life even though her daughter Nanda is now old enough to join the company. 'Is it your theory,' she asks her disapproving cousin, the Duchess,

'that our unfortunate unmarried daughters are to have no intelligent friends?'

'Unfortunate indeed,' cried the Duchess, 'precisely because they're unmarried, and unmarried, if you don't mind my saying so, a good deal *because* they're unmarriageable. Men, after all, the nice ones – by which I mean the possible ones – are not on the lookout for little brides whose usual associates are so up to snuff. It's not their idea that the girls they marry shall already have been pitchforked – by talk and contacts and visits and newspapers, and the way the poor creatures rush about and all the extraordinary things they do – quite into *everything*.' (James, 1899)

Indeed, the knowledge that Nanda acquired proves too much for her young man, who is definitely not 'modern'. The Duchess, by contrast, believes in segregating her daughter even more rigidly than was the English custom: indeed, poor little Aggie is so protected that she appears almost halfwitted.

Innocence, or ignorance as it might more accurately be called, on such a scale, posed its own dangers, when the girl involved had unscrupulous parents, as Kingsley (1857) pointed out in *Two Years Ago*. A young girl who had been married off to an elderly and debauched husband, is now rumoured to be about to run away with a gambler who is only after her money. Who is to blame?

> 'Fathers and mothers who prate hypocritically about keeping their daughters' minds pure; and then abuse a girl's ignorance, in order to sell her to ruin. Let them keep her mind pure, in heaven's name: but let them consider themselves all the more bound in honour to use on her behalf the experience in which she must not share.'

Despite the social pressures to avoid premarital sex, substantial numbers of women were pregnant when they married. Data from selected English parishes covering the period 1800–49 suggests that between one-fifth and two-fifths of first pregnancies were conceived before the wedding (Laslett, 1980). Nevertheless, most couples do not seem to have indulged in sex together until fairly shortly before their marriages.

Although there was premarital pregnancy, and men also had the alternative sexual outlet provided by widespread prostitution, the overall picture is of a people who were willing to postpone regular sexual pleasure, and control sexual desire, in the interests of their future. When the idea of smaller families began to gain acceptance, it did so within a set of values which gave importance to long-term planning and subordinated sexual spontaneity. Neither abstinence nor *coitus interruptus* may have been so difficult to practise then as some modern commentators suggest (Knodel and van der Walle, 1986).

If couples had been sexually active much before their marriages, we might expect that large numbers of 'shotgun' weddings would have moved the average age at marriage downward – and that did not happen. Alternatively, we might guess that the proportion of illegitimate births, out of all live births, would rise during periods when the mean age at marriage was particularly high. In other words, that when couples had to wait longer to marry, there would be more unintended premarital pregnancies.

But one of the most interesting findings of the historical demographers is that, from the sixteenth century onwards, the higher the age at marriage the lower are the ratios of illegitimacy and prenuptial pregnancy. 'The inference might be that when age at marriage rises, sexual nonconformism tends to fall, and that when age at marriage falls, sexual nonconformism rises' (Laslett, 1980). The pressures which made for delays in marrying seem also to have reduced premarital risk-taking.

Another way of looking at 'sexual nonconformism' is to examine the general fertility rate; that is, the annual number of children born to every 1000 women aged 15–49. It can be subdivided into marital fertility and illegitimate fertility rates: again, for England from the sixteenth to the nineteenth century, the two rates are generally in synchrony. Thus, when women were marrying earlier and having more pregnancies, their unmarried sisters were also having more pregnancies; when the age of marriage rose, pregnancies among the unmarried were fewer. However, in the 1840s and 1850s this overall trend changed: the fertility rate fell while illegitimacy rose, indicating some fundamental change in attitudes.

Between 1861 and 1871, levels of illegitimate fertility began to fall, and they had dropped by over 50 per cent by the end of the century, probably as the result of people's increasing ability to avoid pregnancies as the outcome of sexual behaviour (Teitelbaum, 1984).

Many illegitimacies were the result of unforeseen circumstances, rather than of being seduced by a moustache-twirling Sir Jasper, or deliberately flaunting social norms. The biggest group of illegitimate births in England occurred between servants, who were generally planning to marry (Laslett, 1980). Esther Waters (Moore, 1894) is a servant in a household with a racing stable around which all activity and conversation revolves. She falls in love with another servant, William, who proposes to her. They make love, but her extreme fundamentalist religious views make her quarrel with him afterwards. William asks for forgiveness:

'I am very fond of you, Esther, and I will marry you as soon as I have earned enough or won enough money to give you a comfortable home.'

'You are a wicked man; I will never marry you.'

'I am very sorry, Esther. But I am not as bad as you think for. You let your temper get the better of you. So soon as I have got a bit of money together—'

'If you were a good man you would ask me to marry you now.'

'I will if you like, but the truth is that I have only three pounds in the world. I have been unlucky lately—'

'You think of nothing but that wicked betting. Come, let me pass; I'm not going to listen to a lot of lies.'

'After the Leger—'

William, in his desire to get a home together for his bride, was, as we have already seen, not untypical. However, had he known that Esther was already pregnant, it is clear he would have married her without further delay. Only Esther's stubbornness intervenes; and, by the time she herself realises that she is expecting a baby, it is too late. The rejected William has married somebody else.

Among the less-respectable poor, however, marriage might be dispensed with altogether. In the new industrial towns and cities, in particular, churchgoing was far from universal and there were few pressures for social conformity. Thus Mrs Jupp, who keeps a disreputable lodging-house in *The Way of All Flesh* (Butler, 1903) is only 'Mrs' by courtesy, though she has a son; her man is never referred to as a husband, but only as 'the poor dear boy's father'.

Badalia Heronsfoot, a costermonger's daughter, did get married, but

> her husband after two years took to himself another woman, and passed out of Badalia's life, over Badalia's senseless body; for he stifled protest with blows. While she was enjoying her widowhood the baby that the husband had not taken away died of croup, and Badalia was altogether alone. With rare fidelity she listened to no proposals for a second marriage according to the customs of Gunnison Street, which do not differ from those of the Barralong.

Her husband Tom worries that she will follow him and start a fight; not that he minds a fight, but

> he objected to the police-court that would follow, and the orders for maintenance and other devices of a law that cannot understand the simple rule that 'when a man's tired of a woman 'e ain't such a blooming fool as to live with 'er no more, an' that's the long an' short of it'. (Kipling, 1893)

Tom has a child by his new 'wife' and decides to leave her when she is tiresomely pregnant a second time.

Tom's desire for a woman who does not bore him, and his indifference to the children he produces, lead him to a succession of liaisons. But in some ways, his views on marriage do reflect, albeit in a distorted mirror, what many people thought that marriage was 'for'. It does not seem to have been primarily for having children, no matter what the marriage ceremony said; nor was it a matter of fulfilling family strategies. The fact that in England young people were generally responsible for setting up their own households meant that personal choice, rather than parental arrangement, was the basis for most marriages. They came to the marriage as equals, and chose each other for whatever attraction seemed good to them.

What they generally seem to have wanted from each other, both in earlier periods and at this time, was a kind of passionate companionship (MacFarlane, 1986). Love – including sexual desire; but, together with that, a closeness, mutual reliance and communication.

The importance of love – romantic love – had been well-established in Britain for hundreds of years, but its dominance grew with the nineteenth century. The Romantic Movement, which had swept the Continent as well as England, had made individual feelings and desires the test of moral and spiritual behaviour. As Maurois (1953) described the France of George Sand in the 1830s,

> Passion was king, as Reason once had been, and the Irrational was worshipped as a god. . . . Everywhere in France Romanticism was a live issue. The individual was no longer, as he had been in the seventeenth century, a responsible member of a social and religious community. He had become an end in himself, an object of aesthetic contemplation. . . . Reality imitated fiction.

Charlotte Brontë, an adolescent during those years, was equally caught up in the Romantic Movement. Her adoration of Byron and absorption in Scott were influential in her rejection of her own would-be lovers.

> The motives behind Charlotte's rejection of her two suitors . . . lay not, however, in her extravagant conceptions of what the Ideal Lover should be, nor in her exalted notions of what Love should be, but in what she knew love could be for her. It was not the perfection – or imperfection – of the Lover, but the completeness of the feelings he evoked that she judged by. (Gerin, 1967)

Sexual desire was very much a part of the 'completeness of feelings' which people looked for. Charlotte Brontë makes it very clear
why her heroine Jane Eyre refuses her cousin St John Rivers, despite her being destitute, having a high admiration for him and his
missionary cause, and a wish to do something useful in the world:

> 'Can I receive from him the bridal ring, endure all the forms of
> love (which I doubt not that he would scrupulously observe) and
> know that the spirit was quite absent? Can I bear the conscious-
> ness that every endearment he bestows is a sacrifice made on
> principle? No: such a martyrdom would be monstrous. I will
> never undergo it' (Brontë, 1847)

She is quite willing to go with him to India 'as a sister', but not to
endure sexual relations with a man where there is no passion.

An intimate comradeship was also part of the ideal of marriage;
a belief that a couple should share their feelings and their lives, be
friends as well as lovers. One of the most charming long-married
couples in literature must be the retired Admiral and Mrs Croft,
in *Persuasion* (Austen, 1818). Mrs Croft has, whenever possible,
accompanied her husband on all his voyages.

> 'And I do assure you, ma'am,' pursued Mrs Croft, 'that nothing
> can exceed the accommodation of a man of war: I speak, you
> know, of the higher rates. When you come to a frigate, of course,
> you are more confined – though any reasonable woman may be
> perfectly happy in any one of them; and I may safely say, that
> the happiest part of my life has been spent on board a ship. While
> we were together, you know, there was nothing to be feared.
> Thank God! I have always been blessed with excellent health,
> and no climate disagrees with me. A little disordered always the
> first twenty-four hours of going to sea, but never knew what
> sickness was afterwards. The only time I ever really suffered in
> body or mind, the only time that I ever fancied myself unwell, or
> had any idea of danger, was the winter I passed by myself at
> Deal, when the Admiral (Captain Croft then) was in the North
> Seas. I lived in perpetual fright at that time, and had all manner
> of imaginary complaints from not knowing what to do with
> myself, or when I should hear from him next; but as long as we
> could be together, nothing ever ailed me, and I never met with
> the smallest inconvenience.'

Mrs Croft is the cleverer of the pair and in many ways the more capable, but this is of no concern to either. The Admiral, a notoriously poor driver of his horses, frequently overturns their carriage, but Mrs Croft 'makes nothing of it'. In the middle of her conversation with Anne Eliott, to whom they have given a lift, she says,

'– My dear admiral, that post! – we shall certainly take that post.'

But, by coolly giving the reins a better direction herself, they happily passed the danger; and by once afterwards judiciously putting out her hand, they neither fell into a rut, nor ran foul of a dung-cart; and Anne, with some amusement at their style of driving, which she imagined no bad representation of the general guidance of their affairs, found herself safely deposited by them at the cottage.

The Crofts had no children. Had that not been the situation, it is difficult to imagine that Mrs Croft could have pursued her wandering life with her husband: certainly she could not have done so during frequent pregnancies. Nor could she have done so without frequently leaving the children behind, and having to make difficult decisions about where her priorities lay. As the British Empire expanded during the course of Queen Victoria's reign, more and more couples faced with overseas postings or lifetime careers abroad, did have to make such decisions. It was not only because it was the wife's duty to be with her husband that they generally chose the man over the children, but because of the importance of companionship within marriage. Some historians (e.g. Shorter, 1973) suggest that contraception was introduced earlier where marriages were founded on companionship; where a chosen partner, rather than marriage for the sake of the family, was the goal. Certainly, in today's world, companionate marriage in which the partners talk easily to each other is thought to be associated with greater use of family planning.

Marital closeness implied that a wife should be able to share her husband's interests, which she could only do if she had received at least some education. This, in turn, was one of the reasons for the expanding demand for schooling: schooling for girls as well as boys.

William Lovett, the Chartist, was almost entirely self-educated, but nevertheless a keen reader and a political activist. When he married, he was determined that his wife should be a partner in his activities.

I sought to interest my wife, by reading and explaining to her the various subjects that came before us, as well as the political topics of the day. I sought also to convince her that, beyond the pleasure that knowledge conferred on ourselves, we had a duty to perform in endeavouring to use it wisely for others. . . . And in looking back upon this period how often have I found cause for satisfaction that I pursued this course, as my wife's appreciation of my humble exertions has ever been the chief hope to cheer, and the best aid to sustain, me. . . . (1876)

In 1836, Lovett helped to set up the London Working Men's Association, which met in its members' homes, instead of the more usual public houses because those, Lovett considered, too often formed habits and associations which 'mar the domestic happiness'. Besides, he wanted to bring families into the cause of the working men's franchise:

we know not of any means more efficient [to accomplish the goal] than to enlist the sympathies and quicken the intellects, of our wives and children to a knowledge of their rights and duties; for, as in the absence of knowledge, they are the most formidable obstacles to a man's patriotic exertions, so when imbued with it, they will prove his greatest auxiliaries. Read, therefore, talk, and politically and morally instruct your wives and children; let them, as far as possible, share in your pleasures, as they must in your cares; and they will soon learn to appreciate your exertions, and be inspired with your own feelings against the enemies of your country. Thus instructed your wives will spurn instead of promoting you to accept, the base election bribe – your sons will scorn to wear the livery of tyrants – and your daughters will be doubly fortified against the thousand ills to which the children of poverty are exposed. (Lovett, ibid.)

Another implication, both of late marriage and the desire for companionship, was that couples should be fairly close in age. Again, this was not the case in many other parts of the world, but it has been a tradition in Western Europe. Told of Jane Eyre's approaching marriage to Mr Rochester, his housekeeper Mrs Fairfax comments:

'How it will answer I cannot tell: I really don't know. Equality of position and fortune is often advisable in such cases; and there are twenty years of difference in your ages.' (Brontë, Charlotte, 1847)

Both the economic foundation to marriage, and a hint of its companionable virtues, are apparent in Ford Madox Ford's (1931) description of an interview with an elderly pair of poor cottagers in the 1890s. Both partners had been married before – Mrs Spratford three times – and they had produced 31 children between them.

> When you asked Mr Spratford why he married he answered 'Well you see, sir, in a manner of speaking us do be very poor people and us bean't able to afford more than one blanket apiece, and one small fire for each of us, coals do be so dear.' (He got all his coal for nothing from the poor old parson, and so did Mrs Spratt.) 'So if we do marry we do have two blankets atop of us at night and we have one big fire and sit on either side of it.'
> So said Mr Spratford. But when it came to his wife she would scream out:
> 'Why did us marry? Why I, I likes to have a man about the house and a woman looks better like among her neebours if she do have a husband.'

The prestige of being a married woman, at a time when men were in short supply and spinsters – as we saw in a previous chapter – were regarded as permanently non-adult, was considerable. The limited roles available to a spinster also contrasted sharply with the greater possibilities of married life. Mary Lowther was brought up by her elderly aunt, Miss Marrable, who had previously lived with her rector brother until he died; she was then forced to move from her home to a small house where 'the rents were cheap, and here Miss Marrable was able to live, and occasionally to give teaparties'.
With such an example before her, Mary

> was well aware that for her there was but one future mode of life that could be really blessed. She had eyes, and could see; and ears, and could hear. She could make,– indeed, she could not fail to make,– comparisons between her aunt and her dear friend Mrs Fenwick. She saw, and could not fail to see, that the life of one was a starved, thin, poor life,– which, good as it was in its nature, reached but to few persons, and admitted of but few sympathies;

whereas, the other woman, by means of her position as a wife and mother, increased her roots and spread out her branches, so that there was shade, and fruit, and beauty, and a place where the birds might build their nests. (Trollope, 1870)

Despite the attractions of marriage, however, Mary thinks she is determined only to marry where she can love. Nevertheless, before meeting her eventual husband, she tries very hard to learn to love her other suitor, who has everything going for him (including the enthusiastic support of her family and friends) and, when it seems that marriage to her beloved Captain is impossible, she agrees to accept Mr Gilmour.

For Mary is typical of the middle classes, among whom the pursuit of romantic love and companionship came into conflict with those same economic forces which made the age at marriage especially high in this group. A young man's income was unlikely on its own to be sufficient to support a family, but his wife, having never worked, would have nothing to contribute, unless, that is, she had an inheritance or dowry. A prudent match was a necessity. The expansion of the middle classes much increased the numbers who were in this predicament. Besides increasing the numbers of women who did not work before marriage, it resulted in a greater proportion of families within those classes who had no inherited wealth to help provide for the younger generation.

Trollope, who came from the world of the vulnerable and socially aspirant middle classes, summed up the difficulties:

A man born to great wealth may,– without injury to himself or friends,– do pretty nearly what he likes in relation to marriage, always presuming that the wife he selects be of his own rank. He need not marry for money, nor need he abstain from marriage because he can't support a wife without money. And the very poor man, who has no pretension to rank, or standing, other than that which honesty may give him, can do the same. His wife's fortune will consist of the labour of her hands, and in her ability to assist him in his home. But between these there is a middle class of men, who, by reason of their education, are peculiarly susceptible to the charms of womanhood, but who literally cannot marry for love, because their earnings will do no more than support themselves. (Trollope, 1873)

In fact, although Trollope here implies that the upper classes could please themselves, they too were often constrained in their choice of a partner; if not by sheer economic necessity, then by traditional considerations of marriage as a way of adding to wealth or consolidating an alliance. Thus Jane Eyre, when she believes Rochester will marry Blanche Ingram, ruminates:

> It surprised me when I first discovered that such was his intention: I had thought him a man unlikely to be influenced by motives so commonplace in his choice of a wife; but the longer I considered the position, education, &c., of the parties, the less I felt justified in judging or blaming either him or Miss Ingram for acting in conformity to the ideas and principles instilled into them, doubtless, from their childhood. All their class held these principles: I supposed, then, they had reasons for holding them, such as I could not fathom. It seemed to me that, were I a gentleman like him, I would take to my bosom only such a wife as I could love; but the very obviousness of the advantages to the husband's own happiness offered by this plan convinced me that there must be arguments against its general adoption of which I was quite ignorant: otherwise I felt sure all the world would act as I wished to act. (Brontë, Charlotte, 1847)

A young aristocrat might not face financial pressure to delay marriage, but his choice of bride was often circumscribed by lack of independent means. He would then be reliant on parental approval of his decision. The Duke of Omnium, one of the richest men in England, is anxious that his son Lord Silverbridge should settle down. So far, the boy (hardly in his twenties) has been 'unfortunate at Eton'; sent down in disgrace from Cambridge; become involved in shady racing circles with the result that he has lost seventy thousand pounds; and has taken up the wrong side in politics. A worried Duke reasons that

> the surest resource for his son against evil would be in an early marriage. If he would marry becomingly, then might everything still be made pleasant. (Trollope, 1882)

Silverbridge, tiresome as ever, wants to marry an American, which the Duke thinks far from becoming. Although he does eventually give in – and it was part of Trollope's creed that few parents could resist determined children for ever – the fact remains that the path to marriage was not necessarily an easy one even for the Silver-bridges of their time.

The contradiction between individual love and the need for prudence in marriage provides the theme for an overwhelming number of nineteenth-century novels: will true love win out, or will one or other of the young lovers marry for security? Often the author (and reader) are able to avoid the uncomfortable choice by seeing the hero or heroine come into an unexpected legacy or other gift of fortune. In the real world, things were less easy.

For many girls, even the prospect of choice was illusory. Frequently, as Lord Lytton reminds us (1961), a well-bred girl in the latter half of the nineteenth century would marry

> just as a fond and prudent, and, perhaps, pressing mama may advise. Cupid and Dives may or may not be in league, but how simple for the chaperone to be a little sleepy and unobservant in one direction and in one only. Up goes the lorgnon (or maybe it is a lorgnette) for each and every partner on each and every occasion, save in the case of one. . . .

Those women who had earned nothing before marriage, and who were expected to be largely decorative when they had married, were in a poor position to challenge the deep-rooted belief that each party in a marriage should bring a contribution. It was not a belief confined to Britain. In Hungary, even after the First World War, a similar view prevailed among the middle and upper classes.

> If a husband is capable of earning good money, his wife must bring some property to the marriage in order, as it were, to balance the books. Since all the women in these families were relieved almost entirely of all responsibilities other than the supervision of housework, the concept of unpaid work as a contribution to a marriage, so often invoked by modern feminist theory, had little relevance for them. (Riemer, 1992)

However, women who did bring a contribution to the marriage were not encouraged to understand how to manage it, or even what their legal situation with regard to it was. Mrs Prime, the young widow of a clergyman in *Rachel Ray* (Trollope, 1863) has had a proposal of marriage from Mr Prong, and wants to know how far she can retain some independence if she accepts.

She wished much for legal advice, but she made up her mind that was beyond her reach, was beyond her reach as a preliminary assistance. She knew enough of the laws of her country to enable her to be sure that, though she might accept the offer, her own money could so be tied up on her behalf that her husband could not touch the principal of her wealth; but she did not know whether things could be so settled that she might have in her own hands the spending of her income.

Years of using his wife's money as if it were his own made it very easy for a man to forget its origins. The church's insistence that the couple were 'one flesh' helped to undermine the wife's individual contribution – and sometimes even her existence as a separate human being.

In considering a wife as his property, few men went as far as Michael Henchard, who sells his wife – with her child – by auction for five guineas. Such auctions are known to have happened occasionally, and even later than the 1820s in which *The Mayor of Casterbridge* is set but, apart from the proceeding being legally invalid, Hardy suggests that the witnesses in the beer tent may have seen them as going too far.

Perhaps from some little sense of having countenanced an indefensible proceeding, perhaps because it was late, the customers thinned away from the table shortly after this event. (Hardy, 1878)

But, during the century, a number of factors tended to make the general concept of wife-as-property increasingly untenable. The Romantic Movement's emphasis on the individual person marched in tandem with the increasing religious emphasis on the individual soul and its need to be saved. Both had exerted considerable influence in the long struggle to abolish slavery, which was achieved in the British colonies in 1834. The continuance of slavery in the United States until late in the Civil War ensured that this issue remained a crusade for many until 1864, so much so that the war itself was partially an outcome of the immensely popular *Uncle Tom's Cabin* (Stowe, 1852).

Some were quick to see that it was possible to be bought or sold without being an African slave. Mr Rochester tells Jane Eyre that the buyer, as well as the 'slave' are corrupted by the process:

'Hiring a mistress is the next worst thing to buying a slave; both are often by nature and always by position, inferior; and to live familiarly with inferiors is degrading. I now hate the recollection of the time I passed with Celine, Giacinta, and Clara.' (Brontë, Charlotte, 1847)

After the discovery of Rochester's mad wife, when he begs Jane to live with him, her refusal is based less on any moral absolute than the certainty that were she to do so he would come to have the same contempt for both of them.

A mistress was a kept woman, but how different was her position from that of many wives? Irene married Soames Forsyte because he kept asking her; because her widowed stepmother resented her cost and presence at home; because Soames was an excellent match and no others came along. She remains, however, determined to keep a private core.

Soames only experienced a sense of exasperation amounting to pain, that he did not own her as it was his right to own her, that he could not, as by stretching out his hand to that rose, pluck her and sniff the very secrets of her heart.

Out of his other property, out of all the things he had collected, his silver, his pictures, his houses, his investments, he got a secret and intimate feeling; out of her he got none.

... He had married this woman, conquered her, made her his own, and it seemed to him contrary to the most fundamental of all laws, the law of possession, that he could do no more than own her body – if indeed he could do that, which he was beginning to doubt. (Galsworthy, 1906)

Poor Soames desperately wants love and companionship from Irene; he has not grasped the fact that ownership precludes it. One suspects that his attitude would have been subtly different if she had been an independently wealthy woman – but then, of course, she would not have married him. Neither, perhaps, would she have had the same attraction for him; he can only love what he believes he can own.

The concept of wife-as-property was further challenged by two legal initiatives. The first, in 1857, was that divorce became a recognised legal process, rather than something which required a special Act of Parliament. For the first time it became possible – though not easy – for couples to achieve an absolute divorce, with a licence to remarry, instead of merely a judicial separation. 'The full consequences of this blow to the concept of indissoluble Christian marriage have yet to be worked out', wrote the Earl of Lytton a century later. One of those consequences was a weakening of the belief in the two parties to a marriage becoming one; the possibility of divorce admitted the fact that separate individuals were involved. The Matrimonial Causes Act also established, for the first time, that a husband had the duty to support his wife and family even after a divorce, thus freeing middle-class women (who had neither training nor, in most cases, any other skills to offer) from abject dependence upon even the most intolerable marriage.

That not only did marriage involve separate individuals, but the right of each of those individuals to independent control of their own affairs, was recognised in the Married Women's Property Act of 1870, which established the right of wives to whatever they brought to a marriage, or subsequently acquired. Under the law, women had not only ceased to be property: they could own it.

These legal developments probably did not initiate changes in the way in which marriages were viewed. A new law more often responds to a substantial shift in public opinion than creates it. Nevertheless, once it has come into being it helps to consolidate that shift, to institutionalise it. Galsworthy believed that by the year 1895, when Soames's aunt Susan dies, significant change in outlook had penetrated even the conservative and established middle classes. Aunt Susan is cremated, the first Forsyte to desert the family grave in Highgate, but this break with tradition is surprisingly easily accepted.

The third reason why Susan's burial made little stir was the most expansive of all. It was summed up daringly by Euphemia, the pale, the thin: 'Well, I think people have a right to their own bodies, even when they're dead'. Coming from a daughter of Nicholas, a Liberal of the old school and most tyrannical, it was a startling remark – showing in a flash what a lot of water had run under bridges since the death of Aunt Ann in '88, just when the proprietorship of Soames over his wife's body was acquiring the uncertainty which had led to such disaster. Euphemia, of course, spoke like a child, and had no experience, for though well over thirty by now, her name was still Forsyte. But, making all allowances, her remark did undoubtedly show expansion of the principle of liberty, decentralization and shift from others to oneself. When Nicholas heard his daughter's remark from Aunt Hester he had rapped out: 'Wives and daughters! There's no end to their liberty in these days. . . .' He had, of course, never really forgiven the Married Women's Property Act, which would so have interfered with him if he had not mercifully married before it was passed. But, in truth, there was no denying the revolt among the younger Forsytes against being owned by others. . . . (Galsworthy, 1906)

Nevertheless, the sense of equality in marital relationship, which had always been predicated by the desire for passionate comrade-ship, was difficult to achieve in marriages where the visible, con-tinuing contributions of each partner were so different. In fiction even less than in fact was the solution proposed of a working wife. A rare instance is Gissing's Nancy Tarrant, who writes a book in the hope of making money; her husband is a struggling journalist. He is immediately appalled:

'We don't want money so badly as all that. I am writing, because I must do something to live by, and I know of nothing else open to me except pen-work. Whatever trash I turned out, I should be justified; as a man, it's my duty to join in the rough-and-tumble for more or less dirty ha'pence. You, as a woman, have no such duty; nay, it's your positive duty to keep out of the beastly scrim-mage.'
    'It seemed to me that I was *doing* something. Why should a woman be shut out from the life of the world?' (Gissing, 1894)

She is told that her contribution is to bring up their child.
    Tarrant's emphasis on the necessity for his wife to keep out of 'the beastly scrimmage' of earning a living reasserts the doctrine of womanly purity. His claim that looking after their baby is her separate-but-equal role in the marriage is an outcome of the growing significance attached to child development which we have already noted. In Chapter 3, we heard his description of the impor-tance of child-rearing, and the rarity of its successful practitioners.
    Many women were presumably delighted at having the value of childcare not only recognised but elevated to the status of a full-time career which made them full participants in the marital equation. The difficulty of fulfilling such a grave responsibility,

should the babies come one after another, was probably, as has already been suggested, an important motive for curtailing family size. And they may have found it easier to discuss the possibility of limiting births once the importance of their work was recognised.

Others, like Nancy, continued to echo their unmarried sisters in wanting to be '*doing*' something. Marriage, as a solution to the frenzy of unused capacities which was embittering single women, was not necessarily enough. In particular, marriages which contained the inherent contradictions between prudence and romance, and between the desire for companionship and a narrowly-circumscribed role for women, were unlikely to provide the fulfilment for which women hoped. Sexual desire was, in such circumstances, probably an early casualty; abstinence would have engendered few regrets.

7
Births and Babies

Sir Walter Elliot, so Jane Austen tells us, read for pleasure only one book, the *Baronetage*; in particular, he could read his own entry with unfailing interest. It is almost equally fascinating – though for different reasons – in the context of this book.

ELLIOT OF KELLYNCH-HALL
Walter Elliot, born March 1, 1760, married, July 15, 1784, Elizabeth, daughter of James Stevenson, Esq. of South Park, in the county of Gloucester; by which lady (who died 1800) he has issue Elizabeth, born June 1, 1785; Anne, born August 8, 1787; a still-born son, Nov 5, 1789; Mary, born Nov 20, 1791. (Austen, 1818)

Jane Austen's imagined Baronet was firmly rooted in reality. Admittedly, he had married at the age of 24, a year younger than the average age of marriage for men during the second half of the eighteenth century (Wrigley and Schofield, 1983) but that is not unexpected, given his comfortable fortune. Another of Jane Austen's characters, Sir Thomas Bertram, tells his niece

'I am an advocate for early marriages, where there are means in proportion, and would have every young man, with a sufficient income, settle as soon after four-and-twenty as he can.' (Austen, 1814)

Sir Walter's first child was born just under a year after the wedding, as was not unusual. Jane Austen herself assumed that marriage would shortly be followed by pregnancy when she wrote to approve her niece Fanny's delay in getting married:

'By not beginning the business of mothering quite so early in life, you will be young in constitution, spirits, figure and countenance, while Mrs William Hammond is growing old by confinements and nursing.' (Hodge, 1972)

Her comments suggest that late marriage was indeed seen partly as a way of limiting childbearing.

Sir Walter's next two children were born after intervals of 26 and 27 months respectively, while the final daughter arrived after a slightly shorter interval of two years. There were no further offspring, though Lady Elliot lived for a further nine years; even without a surviving son it seems quite likely that Sir Walter and his wife had decided that three children were sufficient. We have already noted that the upper classes tended to make that decision at an earlier period in history than others.

Sir Walter may have been a silly man, but he – and his wife – managed to ensure that the children were well-spaced. The timing of each pregnancy suggests that Lady Elliot probably breast-fed the babies; the slightly, but not substantially shorter interval between the dead boy's birth and that of Mary suggests that the couple abstained from sex for a while after each pregnancy as well.

Abstinence – whether temporary between pregnancies or permanent once a couple had the children they wanted – was certainly a fertility-control technique understood by the unmarried Miss Austen. On hearing the news that a relative of her own had just had another baby, she wrote,

> Good Mrs Deedes! – I hope she will get the better of this Marianne, and then I would recommend to her and Mr D. the simple regimen of separate rooms. (Hodge, ibid.)

Other fertility control possibilities are suggested in the contemporary correspondence of the Noels. In September 1781 Mary Noel informed her niece Judith that

> your dear Sister is greatly mended since I came, & as she is certainly with Child, I hope there is no danger of a relapse at present, & I hope proper measures will be taken as soon as she has lain in to prevent a return; but we will talk over these things more at large when I come. . . . (Elwin, 1967)

Unfortunately discretion prevented this older, and more worldly, spinster from elaborating upon the 'proper measures' in a letter.

Demographically, the picture of Sir Walter's family corresponds quite nicely to what is known about fertility behaviour in the past. Even the death of his son fits the pattern, although Lady Elliot's third pregnancy was not especially dangerous. First-born children were at the greatest risk of death and, during the eighteenth century, the eighth or subsequent children also had higher risks of dying (Wrigley and Schofield, ibid.). However, boys everywhere were, and continue, more likely to be still-born or die in infancy than girls. In any case, the possibility of losing any baby was high.

It is thought that the infant mortality rate during the period may have been around 133–165 for every 1000 live births. Those figures indicate that between one in seven and one in six babies died during their first year alone. Childhood deaths were also frequent, so that, in all, almost three out of every ten live-born babies failed to survive to the age of 15. Similar levels of infant and child mortality continued until the 1870s, when child – but not infant – deaths began to decline.

Inevitably some families suffered greater losses, others fewer. Jacob Brattle, the miller in Trollope's *Vicar of Bullhampton* (1870), who is aged about 65 at the time of the story,

> had married the daughter of a neighbouring farmer, and had had some twelve or fourteen children. There were at this time six still living. . . .

By contrast, Mr Toogood, the solicitor in *The Last Chronicle of Barset* (Trollope 1867) describes his family:

> 'I've twelve of 'em living, Mr Crawley – from eighteen years, the eldest – a girl, down to eighteen months the youngest – a boy, and they go in and out, boy and girl, boy and girl, like the cogs of a wheel . . .'.

Although Mr Toogood's phrase 'twelve of them living . . .' suggests that there may have been additional children who did not survive, there cannot have been many. As it is, there is only an average of eighteen months' gap between each of his brood.

The differences in child survival between Mr Brattle's and Mr Toogood's families may have been due, in part, to their very different incomes. Jacob Brattle's mill is not particularly thriving; Mr Toogood, despite his ritual complaints about how much his family costs him, obviously has a comfortable income and can afford treats for them all.

'I comfort myself with the text about the quiver, you know; and I tell them that when they've eaten up the butter, they'll have to take their bread dry.'

'I trust the young people take your teaching in a proper spirit.'

'I don't know much about spirit. There's spirit enough. My second girl, Lucy, told me that if I came home today without tickets for the pantomime I shouldn't have any dinner allowed me. That's the way they treat me. But we understand each other at home. We're all pretty good friends there, thank God. And there isn't a sick chick among the boiling.'

The text about the quiver is from Psalms 127: 'Lo, children are an heritage of the Lord: . . . Happy is the man that hath his quiver full of them.'

Deaths of infants and children were more common among the poor, as one would expect; they were also more common in the crowded cities. Poverty and ignorance combined to defeat many struggling lives. Looey Perrott, ten months old, has the misfortune to have been born into one of the worst of London's slums. When her brother returns to the single room which is the family home, and asks for food, he is told there may be some bread.

The boy rummaged and found a crust. Gnawing at this, he crossed to where the baby lay. "Ullo, Looey,' he said, bending and patting the muddy cheek. "Ullo!'

The baby turned feebly on its back, and set up a thin wail. Its eyes were large and bright, its tiny face was piteously flea-bitten and strangely old. 'Why, she's 'ungry, mother,' said Dicky Perrott, and took the little thing up.

He sat on a small box, and rocked the baby on his knees, feeding it with morsels of chewed bread. (Morrison, 1896)

Accidentally knocked over in a street fight, Looey suffers a head injury and gradually becomes feverish and 'rum about the eyes'. When even a special meal of boiled tripe and beer which is offered to her meets only with 'choking rejection' the family decides that she must be ill, and take her to a dispensary, one of several

kept by a medical man who lived away from them, and bothered himself as little about them as was consistent with banking the takings and signing the death-certificates.

The medical student he employs has two drugs for every occasion: turkey rhubarb and sulphuric acid. For a sixpenny fee, Looey gets rhubarb and the family also buy 'a fluid bought at a chandler's shop, and called milk'. A little while later, Looey dies.

However, wealthy families were not immune to child deaths, either, and sometimes contributed directly to the risks their children encountered. Mr Gresham of Greshamsbury and his aristocratic wife in *Dr Thorne* (Trollope, 1858) have ten children in twelve years. 'Some of these little girls were sickly, some very sickly.' Selina coughed, Helena was hectic, poor Sophy's spine was weak, and Matilda's appetite was gone. Lady Arabella was not an indifferent mother, and

> her poor weak darlings were carried about from London to Brighton to some German baths, from the German baths back to Torquay, and thence – as regarded the four we have named – to that bourne from whence no further journey could be made under the Lady Arabella's directions.

The four all die in a single year, and then Lady Arabella has twins

> weak, delicate, frail little flowers . . . whom men look on as fated to follow their sisters with quick steps.

The fact that there were ten births in twelve years was, in itself, probably sufficient to explain the sad fate of several of the Gresham children. Studies from all over the world have shown that closely-spaced births are very much more likely to lead to death – either the death of the new baby, or of its previous sibling; and this remains true even when other factors, like the parents' income or education, are taken into account (Hobcraft *et al.*, 1983).

Trollope, however, adds a further reason for the children's poor health; one which also suggests just why the Greshams had so many children in such a short time:

> Of course, Lady Arabella could not suckle the young heir herself. Ladies Arabella never can. They are gifted with the power of being mothers, but not nursing-mothers. Nature gives them bosoms for show, but not for use. So Lady Arabella had a wet nurse.

We learn that the nurse has come from Lady Arabella's family estates, where a supply of such women was 'kept up on the lord's demesne for the family use'. Too late, it emerged that despite these magnificent antecedents she 'was fond of brandy'.

Here again the distant influence of Rousseau can be heard. His attacks on fashionable women's refusal to breastfeed, and his awareness of the extra dangers to which wet-nursing exposed a baby, were immensely influential not only in France but throughout Europe (Morel, 1991).

, French parents sent their children to the nurse's home, and left them there for a year or two, if they survived. Many did not: the process might involve a long journey with a careless carter, and their destinations were frequently sordid. Emma Bovary's wet-nurse was at least a local woman, but the detailed description of her surroundings does much to explain the high French infant mortality.

It was a little low house with a brown tiled roof; a string of onions was hanging down from the attic window. Some faggots propped against the thorn hedge surrounded a bed of lettuce, a few head of lavender, and some sweet peas trained on sticks. Little runnels of dirty water trickled over the grass, and all around were various nondescript rags, woollen stockings, a red calico night-dress, a large thick sheet spread out on top of the hedge. The squeak of the gates brought out the nurse, carrying in one arm a baby that she was suckling. With her other hand she dragged along a puny little boy with scabs all over his face, the son of a Rouen draper, left in the country by parents too engrossed with their business.

'Come in,' she said. 'Your baby's over there, asleep.'

The downstairs bedroom, the only one there was, had a large uncurtained bed standing against the far wall, while a kneading-trough took up the side by the window, one pane of which was stuck together with a blue paper star. In the corner behind the door, under the sink, was a row of boots with shiny hobnails and a bottle of oil with a feather in its mouth. Amid the gunflints, candle-ends and bits of tinder on the dusty mantelpiece was propped a Mattieu Laensberg almanac. The final unnecessary touch was added to the room by a picture of Fame blowing her trumpets, which had presumably been cut out of some advertisement for scent, and was nailed to the wall with half a dozen beads. (Flaubert, 1857)

Emma's husband might be a doctor but he was nevertheless apparently quite unperturbed at leaving his daughter in such a place. Emma's lover Leon merely thought what a strange sight it was to see Emma, 'that lovely woman in her nankeen dress in these squalid surroundings'.

Colette confirms that the sufferings of French babies continued throughout the nineteenth century. Describing a country doctor's practice of around 1890 she wrote

> Every month he had the duty of inspecting all the babies in the region and he tried to drop in unexpectedly on their wet or dry nurses. Those expeditions used to ruin his appetite. How many babies we found alone in empty houses, tied to their fetid cradles with handkerchiefs and safety pins, while their heedless guardians worked in the fields. . . . (Colette, 1937)

Wet-nursing seems to have been less common in Britain than it was in France and those women who did employ a wet-nurse appear to have more often done so at home, instead of boarding the baby out as the French did. The more widespread practice of breastfeeding in Britain is thought to account for its lower levels of infant mortality than those which existed in various other Western European countries (Woods *et al.*, 1989). But wherever women could not, or would not, feed their own babies, the wet-nurse was all too frequently drunk or diseased. A wet-nurse represented a threat to which a more wary mother than Lady Arabella would have been alert.

Thus when Esther Waters becomes a wet-nurse in a desperate effort to support her illegitimate child, her employer demands that she is examined by a doctor beforehand. Once in the house, Esther noticed, too,

> that she was never allowed out alone, and that her walks were limited to just enough exercise to keep her in health.

Esther's boarded-out baby becomes ill but she is not allowed to go and visit it; her employer informs her that

> 'When the baby is well, and the doctor is satisfied there is no danger of infection, you can bring it here – once a month will be sufficient.' (Moore, 1894)

The frequency with which, before the current century, their children died seemed, to most people, inevitable. Which is not to say that parents did not suffer real grief; the letter which Sir Walter Raleigh wrote to his wife, when their son Wat was killed at the age of 22, for example, carries its anguish across four centuries:

> I was loth to write, because I know not how to comfort you; And God knows I never knew what sorrow meant till now. All that I can say to you is, that you must obey the will and providence of God, and remember that the Queen's Majesty bare the loss of the Prince Henry with a magnanimous heart, and the Lady Harrington of her only son. Comfort your heart (Deare Bess); I shall sorrow for us both: and I shall sorrow the less because I have not long to sorrow, because I have not long to live. . . . The Lord bless you and Comfort you, that you may bear patiently the death of your most valiant son. (Raleigh, 1618)

All he can suggest to his 'Deare Bess' is endurance – the strength to bear the disaster – and submission to God's will; he is very well aware that her pain, like his own, cannot be lightened.

It might be argued that the Raleighs' desolation came from having seen their child safely through his childhood, only to lose him after they had come to share many loving years. Certainly, the deaths of babies and small children do not seem to have caused such intensity of feeling, if only because such deaths were so terribly common as to be almost anticipated.

The dead often seem to have been only marginally distinguished from the living, who might join them in the next world at any time. The kneeling family groups on sixteenth- and seventeenth-century tombs portrayed all a couple's children, not merely the survivors who were around when the sculptor did his work. Hogarth's famous painting of the children of Daniel Graham, Apothecary to the Chelsea Hospital, included one who had already died; in Central Europe painters indicated the deceased members included in a family group portrait only by placing a small cross above their heads.

Laurie Lee describes that same all-embracing concept of the family still surviving in Spain in the 1930s, where it was presented to him by

> the deaf-mute boy Alonso . . . whose restless face and body built up images like a silent movie. He described his family in mime, patting their several heads, and suddenly one could see them in

a row beside him – his handsome father, his coughing consump-
tive mother, fighting brothers, and sly younger sister. There was
also a sickly baby, its head lolling back, and two dead ones, packed
into little boxes – the boy set their limbs stiffly, sprinkled them
with prayers, closed their eyes, and laid them away with a shrug.
(Lee, 1969)

Parish records quite often show a subsequent child being given
the same names as its deceased brother or sister. When the dis-
tinctions between the living and the dead were so blurred, that
seems to have been more an attempt to reincarnate the lost child –
to have it live on through a new sibling – than an indication that the
dead child had been forgotten. While 'the family' was undoubtedly
more important than the fate of every child it included, each child
had its own significance, even in retrospect, as a family member.
Only as a family member, however: its individuality went for little.

Changing perceptions of childhood, which we have already seen
emerge from the spread of Evangelicalism and nonconformism,
as well as from Rousseau, inevitably had an impact on the way in
which child deaths were viewed. Those who believed that the world
was a dark and wicked place tried to convince themselves that, by
dying, the child had escaped from the contaminations of sin.

Jane Austen, who had grown up among liberal eighteenth-
century clergy, could hardly endorse such a claim. When Mrs Price,
in *Mansfield Park* (1814), says of her dead daughter

'Poor little sweet creature! Well, she was taken away from evil to
come.'

it is perfectly clear that she has little real feeling about the tragedy.
Later on, Jane Austen is even more explicit about what she saw as
indifference hypocritically masquerading as pious resignation:

Three or four Prices might have been swept away, any or all,
except Fanny and William, and Lady Bertram would have thought
little about it; or perhaps might have caught from Mrs Norris's
lips the cant of it being a very happy thing, and a great blessing
to their poor dear sister Price to have them so well provided for.

Two generations later, Kingsley (1857), while disapproving of the
doctrine, is prepared to accept that Grace Harvey is genuine in her

outpourings of gratitude (when the first natural tears had dried), as often as one of her little lambs was 'delivered out of the miseries of this sinful world'.

Both those who thought that the wicked world corrupted the innocent, and those who believed that even the smallest child was dangerously full of original sin, were concerned first and foremost with the child's soul. So was the Princess Royal, in raptures about her first pregnancy, but her mother, Queen Victoria, was not convinced:

> What you say of the pride of giving life to an immortal soul is very fine, dear, but I own I cannot enter into that; I think much more of our being like a cow or a dog at such moments, when our poor nature becomes so very animal & unecstatic. . . . (Longford, 1964)

But for those who did see childbearing in terms of an immortal soul, the question of getting that soul safely to Heaven was critical. No longer, in the nineteenth century, was it taken for granted that the family would meet in another world; now parents and friends hung on the words of the dying child for reassurance that it was, indeed, going to a better place.

The child Jane Eyre creeps into the bedroom where Helen is dying:

> 'Are you going somewhere, Helen? Are you going home?'
> 'Yes; to my long home – my last home. . . . Jane, your little feet are bare; lie down and cover yourself with my quilt' . . . After a long silence, she resumed, still whispering –
> 'I am very happy, Jane; and when you hear that I am dead, you must be sure and not grieve: there is nothing to grieve about. We all must die one day, and the illness which is removing me is not painful; it is gentle and gradual; my mind is at rest. I leave no one to regret me much: I have only a father, and he is lately married, and will not miss me. By dying young I shall escape great sufferings. I had not qualities or talents to make my way very well in the world: I should have been continually at fault.'
> 'But where are you going to, Helen? Can you see? Do you know?'
> 'I believe; I have faith; I am going to God.' (Brontë, Charlotte, 1847)

Charlotte Brontë wrote out of her remembered anguish at the death of her sister Maria. Dickens too – in his innumerable death-bed-scenes – drew upon his personal grief at the death of Mary Hogarth,

> Young, beautiful and good,
> God in his Mercy
> Numbered her with his Angels
> At the early age of
> Seventeen

Most famous was his account of the death of Little Nell (*The Old Curiosity Shop*, 1841):

> 'She seemed a creature fresh from the hand of God . . . so shall we know the angels in their majesty, after death'

but other novels repeated the same theme. Paul Dombey puts his arms around his sister Floy and tells her that he can see their dead parent.

> 'Mama is like you, Floy. I know her by the face. But tell them that the print on the stairs at school is not divine enough. The light about the head is shining on me as I go!' . . . And look upon us, angels of young children, with regards not quite estranged, when the swift rivers bear us to the ocean! (Dickens, 1848)

For such deathbed-scenes the child had to have reached a certain age: it must be able to speak its edifying words. Despite the Princess Royal's talk of giving birth to an immortal soul, few people seem to have thought that the soul of a small baby required much attention.

During the eighteenth century there had begun to be an increasing gap between birth and baptism, and an increasing tendency to fail to record the burial of children who died unchristened. These trends have proved a serious problem to historical demographers using parish records to estimate infant mortality (Wrigley and Schofield, 1983). Equally important, from our point of view, is that declining urgency about baptising a new baby and ensuring it Christian burial, suggests a shift in popular thinking. Parents may have become less interested in the fate of an embryonic soul, or more confident that God would not overlook this least of His little ones even without the Church's intercession.

The Registration Act of 1836 did not make registration of births compulsory in England, and it entirely ignored stillbirths, which were also ignored in the later Act of 1874, though it did make birth-registration obligatory. Parents, midwives and doctors tended to lump together babies who were stillborn and those who had survived a few hours or even days; they saw no reason to give them an official, registered existence. Besides, it was considerably cheaper to bury a stillborn child.

> In 1893 St Pancras Burial Board charged 7 shillings and 8 pence for burying a live-born as against 2 shillings and sixpence for a stillborn, and by paying an undertaker to stuff a stillborn secretly inside a coffin with an adult, the cemetery fees could be avoided altogether. Stillborns were dumped in exposed places, and not unusually, and quite legally, buried in people's own back gardens to avoid burial costs. If a baby lived for a few hours, it was still casually treated as a stillborn. (Rose, 1986)

This practice, despite increasing official concern, continued into the current century. When Laurie Lee entered the world around the beginning of the First World War it was

> in doubt and silence, a frail little lifeless lump; and the midwife, after one look at my worn-out face, said I wouldn't last the day. Everybody agreed, including the doctor, and they just waited for me to die.
>
> My Mother, however, while resigned to my loss, was determined I should enter heaven. She remembered those tiny anonymous graves tucked away under the churchyard laurels, where quick-dying infants – behind the vicar's back – were stowed secretly among the jam-jars. She said the bones of her son should rest in God's own ground and not rot with those pitiful heathens. So she summoned the curate, who came and called out my Adam, baptised me with a tea-cup, admitted me to the Church, and gave me three names to die with. (Lee, 1959)

Those pitiful heathens, tucked away among the jam-jars, were clearly a quite different order of being from the angelic child lisping its deathbed words.

Babies in the abstract too – plural babies – were seldom recognised as an intimation of immortality. They might be an investment, or – more frequently – herald a problem. If they were an investment, it was more for the earnings they quickly brought in than as representing security in the parents' old age.

Among factory workers, parents were believed, as we have already noted, to keep the older children at home for their wages. When Harriet, the weaver's daughter in *Sybil* refuses to contribute any longer and runs away from home, her mother is furious; she seems to see the girl as a kind of serf. 'You have let the girl escape . . . That wicked Harriet!' (Disraeli, 1845)

But she must have known that it was only a matter of time before Harriet did get away: the whole English tradition of children working to support their own marriage and family supported her.

In a different social class, but also with financial difficulties, Montague Dartie has greater hopes for the future as well as the present. He sees his children as a way of getting him the best of everything:

No sounder principle on which a man can base his life, whose father-in-law has a very considerable income, and a partiality for his grandchildren.

With his not unable eye, Dartie had spotted this weakness in James the very first year after little Publius's arrival (an error); he had profited by his perspicacity. Four little Darties were now a sort of perpetual insurance. (Galsworthy, 1906)

In rural areas, gentry anxious to ensure a supply of labour might even offer incentives to the virtuous poor to have large families. One of the Casterbridge rustics recalls, in the 1850s, Mrs Cuxsom's background:

'Your mother was a very good woman – I can mind her. She were rewarded by the Agricultural Society for having begot the greatest number of healthy children without parish assistance, and other virtuous marvels.'

' 'Twas that that kept us so low upon ground – that great hungry family.'

'Ay. Where the pigs be many the wash runs thin.' (Hardy, 1886)

These particular yokels were obviously not impressed. Contemporary comments are overwhelmingly against very large families, generally because of the difficulty of providing for them: Trollope's Mr Toogood, happily quoting the Psalmist's approbation of the man who has his quiver full of children, is a rare exception; and, of course, his name is significant.

Most people took the Biblical injunction to be fruitful and multiply – but only as far as five or six children, rather than up to any biological maximum. Even Montague Dartie thinks four children are quite enough insurance.

As the Rev. George Austen's family increased, his brother-in-law, surveying the new arrivals of 1765, 1766, 1768 and 1771, wrote, 'I fear George will find it easier to get a family than provide for them.' (Hodge, 1972) George's solution, as we noted in the first chapter, was to unload one of the boys on to a childless relative. Perhaps influenced by her experience of coming from a large family with straitened means, his daughter Jane painted depressing pictures of the likely results of unchecked fertility. Mrs Jennings, contemplating a sad future for Lucy Steele and Edward Ferrars, who, unable to get a church living, will have to marry on a curate's stipend, prophesies

'Then they will have a child every year! and Lord help 'em! how poor they will be!' (Austen, 1811)

The declining welcome extended to later children is captured by another of Hardy's yokels:

'You be bound to dance at Christmas because 'tis the time of year; you must dance at weddings because 'tis the time of life. At christenings folk will even smuggle in a reel or two, if 'tis no further on than the first or second chiel . . .'. (Hardy, 1878)

It is echoed in the story of the Greshams – whose problems with sickly children we met earlier – who began their married life with a comfortable estate. Poor management and Lady Arabella's grand ideas contributed to its decline and their increasing debts, but so too, says Trollope, did those ten children in twelve years. Their firstborn was a son, and they celebrated with bonfires, roasted oxen, and the customary paraphernalia of joy usual to rich Britons. . . . But when the tenth baby, and the ninth little girl, was brought into the world, the outward show of joy was not so great. (Trollope, 1858)

Poverty compounded by the demands of a large family was not only an evil in itself, it was seen as undermining any possibility of independence or dignity. Mrs Price married in opposition to her family's wishes and quarrelled with them.

By the end of eleven years, however, Mrs Price could no longer afford to cherish pride or resentment, or to lose one connection that might possibly assist her. A large and still increasing family, an husband disabled for active service, but not the less equal to company and good liquor, and a very small income to support their wants, made her eager to regain the friends she had so carelessly sacrificed; and she addressed Lady Bertram in a letter which spoke so much contrition and despondence, such a super-fluity of children, and such a want of almost everything else, as could not but dispose them all to a reconciliation. (Austen, 1814)

The humiliation entailed by a superfluity of children and a want of almost everything else is all too apparent in Trollope's Mr Quiverful, with his fourteen children and four hundred pounds a year, who is forced to be 'cringingly civil' to the odious Mr Slope in the hope of preferment.

The impossible task of bringing up as ladies and gentlemen four-teen children on an income which was insufficient to give them with decency the common necessities of life had had an effect on him not beneficial either to his spirit or his keen sense of honour. . . .

Mrs Quiverful has become still more desperate. In her struggle to provide for them she

had given over being shamefaced, and, in some things, had given over being decent. . . . (Trollope, 1857)

Apart from the financial burden which a large family imposed, women at least were acutely aware of the burden which childbearing itself imposed. Poor Queen Victoria, who multiplied more than most, certainly saw no need to interpret the Bible too literally. Replying to King Leopold, who had congratulated her on the birth of a daughter and wished her many more babies, she wrote

> I think, dearest Uncle, you cannot really wish me to be the *'mamma d'une nombreuse famille'*, . . . men never think, at least seldom think, what a hard task it is for us women to go through this very often. (Longford, 1964)

One of the Queen's greatest gifts to the women of England was to pioneer the use of chloroform in childbirth, rejecting the age-old belief that pain in labour was part of a woman's divinely-appointed lot. 'In sorrow shalt thou bring forth children', said the Bible; even after the advent of chloroform, pregnancy and childbearing were all too often an unhappy business. And it was no less dangerous than it had been for Sophia Curzon, a couple of generations earlier.

Sophia, the niece about whose health Mary Noel had been concerned in 1781, had given birth to her second child in January of the same year. She had always been a sickly girl; whether she was, or was not, really pregnant again, as Miss Noel was first told, is unclear from succeeding letters reporting contrary doctors' diagnoses: she was, however, dead within a year (Elwin, 1967).

Maternal mortality was very high; the reported rate for England and Wales in 1847 – the first year for which there are reasonable statistics – was six maternal deaths for every 1000 live births, and even this is a considerable underestimate (Smith, 1979). (Today, for comparison, fewer than one woman dies during pregnancy and childbirth in England and Wales for every 10 000 live births.)

Not surprisingly, pregnant women thought about the likelihood of dying, and often composed a kind of testament for their existing children or for the coming child. They had nothing else to leave, and feared that even their memory would not long remain, especially if the husband remarried.

The orphaned Philip Carey goes to live with his uncle and aunt; a week later, an envelope arrives containing a dozen photographs of his dead mother. She had been lying in bed one day when

> suddenly Mrs Carey felt alone in the world. A great fear seized her that she would not recover from the confinement which she was expecting in a fortnight. Her son was nine years old. How could he be expected to remember her? She could not bear to

think that he would grow up and forget her utterly; and she had loved him so passionately, because he was weakly and deformed, and because he was her child. She had no photographs of herself taken since her marriage, and that was ten years before. She wanted her son to know what she looked like at the end. He could not forget her then, not forget utterly. . . . (Maugham, 1915)

She dresses with special care and great difficulty and struggles to a photographer, where she is so evidently ill that he suggests postponing the sitting, but she insists on staying to the end. She dies shortly afterwards, giving birth to a stillborn child.

Other mothers composed letters. Christina Pontifex writes a highflown and sanctimonious epistle, which mainly tells her two sons to be dutiful to their father and to follow God through the strait gate which leads to eternal life. The narrator says that the letter was found many years afterwards, on Christina's death,

among papers which she had repeatedly and carefully arranged, and with the seal broken. This I am afraid shows that Christina had read it and thought it too creditable to be destroyed when the occasion that had called it forth had gone by. . . . From enquiries I have made I have satisfied myself that most mothers write letters like this shortly before their confinements, and that about fifty per cent keep them afterwards as Christina did. (Butler, 1903)

The editor's footnote to my edition of *Ernest Pontifex* says that the letter

is taken almost word for word from one written by Butler's mother as she lay seriously ill in 1841, but not received by her son until after her death in 1873, just as he was writing this part of the book. (Howard, 1965)

Butler resented his parents and his horrible childhood under their rule, and was not inclined to see anything touching about his mother's posthumous message. The letter, sadly, does reflect his mother's unattractive character. All the same, the fears which led her to write, and the impulse to keep the memorial to those fears, have a certain pathos when one recalls the real risks women like her endured.

Those who survived childbearing were often worn down by frequent births. Many suffered what is now called 'maternal depletion syndrome' – the synergism of poor diet, anaemia and frequent minor illnesses, exacerbated by repeated childbirth and breastfeeding. Among other things, it is thought to have contributed to the high rates of tuberculosis – and deaths from TB – among women in the nineteenth century. Other women, like the unfortunate Queen Victoria, suffered severe post-natal depression, and referred to pregnancy as 'the ONLY thing I *dread*'.

Altogether, it was understandable that women wished to postpone childbearing or minimise its frequency, and that men too might also have their reservations about the process. At the very least, children ended one's youth. Thus, when Caroline Waddington asks her lover to wait for three years and get established before they marry, his friend agrees.

'Wait, my dear fellow, with a little patience; you'll have lots of time before you for married troubles. What's the use of a man having half-a-score of children round him just when he is beginning to enjoy life? It is that that Miss Waddington thinks about; though, of course, she can't tell you so.' (Trollope, 1859)

By the 1880s, in which period The *Man of Property* is set, even the established and conservative Forsytes are opting for smaller families and linking that decision to the health of their womenfolk. At Swithin's dinner table, the casual conversation includes the comment,

'Winifred? she's got too many children. Four, isn't it? She's as thin as a lathe!' (Galsworthy, 1906)

Winifred was Montague Dartie's wife. The statement suggests that Montague's infant insurance policies were excessive. It also suggests that the assumption that couples could choose for themselves about childbearing had become established. Even poor old James Forsyte, deeply concerned that Soames is losing his wife Irene to Bosinney, says

'Well, I don't know; I expect the worst. This is what comes of having no children. I knew how it would be from the first. They never told me they didn't mean to have any children – nobody tells me anything!'

James may disapprove of childlessness as a threat to a marriage, but he is well aware that it has been a deliberate choice.

Whatever caused this dramatic shift in attitudes to childbearing, it seems to have had little to do with people's confidence about the survival of those children they chose to have. Conventional demographic theory holds that declines in fertility within marriage follow declines in infant and child mortality: in other words, people begin to limit the size of their families when they become reasonably sure that the babies they have will live.

Unfortunately the data – for England and Wales at least – do nothing to support this proposition. Fertility began its fall in the 1870s and had reached a 10 per cent reduction by 1892. Meanwhile, during the last quarter of the nineteenth century, the infant mortality rate did not fall, and may possibly even have increased. It was only after 1900 that there was any improvement in the rate of infant deaths.

From the mid-1860s, there had begun to be improvements in the prospects for children who survived infancy: death rates of those aged 2, 3 and 4 also began their long-term decline (Woods *et al.* 1988/9). But few parents, or prospective parents of the time could have recognised that was happening; it is only retrospectively that one can be confident about such a trend and in any case it was probably overshadowed in people's perceptions by the continuing vulnerability of infants. The desire, and the determination, by English couples to limit family size was independent of any change in mortality rates.

8
Fertility Limitation

Young Sophia Curzon in 1781 wrote to her aunt about a mutual acquaintance:

> But how terrible to have eight Children . . . after a certain number they ought always to be drowned like puppys. . . . (Elwin, 1967)

From at least the seventeenth century, the English have had comparatively small numbers of children. Thus, between 1600 and 1799, the average Frenchwoman had between one and two more births than her English counterpart (Wrigley and Schofield, 1983.)

The evidence for such a difference is based upon parish registers, which recorded baptisms as well as marriages and deaths. However, a certain number of babies never reached the font; if they were stillborn, or died before being christened there was unlikely to be any record of their brief existence. As a result it was not difficult to get rid of an unwelcome infant; like puppies, they were discreetly disposed of. High-Place Hall in Hardy's Casterbridge was a useful site for all sorts of shady transactions:

> The position of the queer old door and the odd presence of the leering mask suggested one thing above all others as appertaining to the mansion's past history – intrigue. By the alley it had been possible to come unseen from all sorts of quarters in the town – the old play-house, the old bull-stake, the old cock-pit, the pool wherein nameless infants had been used to disappear. High-Place Hall could boast of its conveniences undoubtedly. (Hardy, 1886)

Outright infanticide of this type was probably comparatively uncommon and largely confined, as the phrase 'nameless infants' suggests, to illegitimate babies.

Until well on in the nineteenth century, however, its occurrence seems to have been taken for granted. A matter-of-fact recognition of infanticide, as well as some humour about it, can be found in an early (1797) version of the popular nursery rhyme

There was a little old woman, and she liv'd in a shoe,
She had so many children, she didn't know what to do.
She crumm'd 'em some porridge without any bread;
And she borrow'd a beetle, and she knocked 'em all o' the head.
Then out whent th' old woman to bespeak 'em a coffin
And when she came back, she found 'em all a-loffeing.

The Opies (1952) suggest a folklore significance to the rhyme, and point out that a shoe was symbolic of what was personal to a woman until marriage; throwing a shoe after a wedding couple may have signified a wish for fruitfulness in the union. Here, as we saw in the previous chapter, it is noticeable that the English do not appear to have thought unending fruitfulness a blessing.

Other reluctant parents simply abandoned an unwanted child. One might trip over a baby in a Church porch or on a doorstep, or even, like Squire Allworthy, be

preparing to step into bed, when upon opening the cloaths, to his great surprize, he beheld an infant, wrapt up in some coarse linnen. . . . (Fielding, 1749)

That infant – Tom Jones – incidentally provides a nice example of the psychic fluidity of families discussed in the first chapter; his later sexual exploits lead to his fear that he has unwittingly slept with his mother, and he eventually turns out to be the illegitimate nephew of Squire Allworthy himself.

All over Europe foundling hospitals had opened to deal with the problem of abandoned children; some, like the Hospital of the Innocents in Florence, in buildings of considerable magnificence. The charitable supported these institutions, and got their servants from them. Not only single mothers abandoned their babies; families did too. Corsini (1977) examined the records for the Florence foundling hospital in the eighteenth and early nineteenth centuries, and found that among the babies who were brought in from existing families, higher-parity children were abandoned in higher proportions. He describes foundlings as

A phenomenon which for the Italian experience in particular but for Europe in general seems to increase progressively from the beginning of the 16th century until around the middle of the 19th; it then declines and disappears.

In Florence, some of the children were not really 'abandoned' but left by parents who – for reasons of illness or economic hardship – might initially hope to reclaim them. It was a hope not often fulfilled; only just over a quarter ever returned to the parental home.

Although the foundling phenomenon never completely disappeared, in Britain by the end of the nineteenth century it had become sufficiently unusual and old-fashioned to be treated as a joke.

Jack: I don't actually know who I am by birth. I was . . . well, I was found.

Lady Bracknell: Found!

Jack: The late Mr Thomas Cardew, an old gentleman of a very charitable disposition, found me, and gave me the name of Worthing, because he happened to have a first-class ticket for Worthing in his pocket at the time. Worthing is a place in Sussex. It is a seaside resort.

Lady Bracknell: Where did the charitable gentleman who had a first-class ticket for this season resort find you?

Jack (Gravely.): In a handbag.

Lady Bracknell: A handbag?

(Wilde, 1899)

Charitable people like Mr Thomas Cardew could assume responsibility for any stray infant without legal or bureaucratic problems. The reclusive miser Silas Marner (Eliot, 1861) is quite free (despite his apparent unsuitability for bringing up a child) to 'adopt' little Eppie who crawls into his cottage when her abandoned mother dies nearby in the snow. Until 1926 in England, and 1930 in Scotland, with the passing of the relevant Adoption Acts, there was no concept of adoption as we now know it, with full legal parental rights and duties over a strange child. The word 'adoption' meant fostering; anybody could give or sell a child to somebody else and anybody could take on a child – without it acquiring any legal rights within a new family.

Other children whose parents could, or would, not undertake their support were sent to baby-farmers, who advertised in large numbers throughout the nineteenth century. Many – like Esther Waters, who places her illegitimate baby in the care of Mrs Spires, at six shillings a week, while she hires herself out as a wet-nurse – were doing the best they could for the child. Others were more ambivalent. Mrs Spires says,

'You girls is all alike; yer thinks of nothing but yer babies for the first few weeks, then yer tires of them, the drag on you is that 'eavy – I knows yer – and then yer begins to wish they 'ad never been born, or yer wishes they had died afore they knew they was alive. I don't say I'm not often sorry for them, poor little dears, but they takes less notice than you'd think for, and they're better out of the way, and that's a fact: it saves a lot of trouble hereafter. I often do think that to neglect them, to let them go off quiet, that I be their best friend; not wilful neglect, yer know, but what is a woman to do with ten or a dozen, and I often 'as as many? I am sure they'd thank me for it.' (Moore, 1894)

Baby-farmers also varied in what they were prepared to undertake: some provided genuine and adequate foster-homes; a large number of others simply took the money and neglected and starved the infants; a few straightforwardly murdered their charges (Rose, 1987). Those who took a child for a fixed sum had no incentive to keep it alive, as everybody involved was aware. Mrs Spires, with her careful distinction between 'neglect' and 'wilful neglect', likes to see herself as innocent. But, convinced that Esther is repenting of her decision to bring the child up, she proceeds to suggest taking it off Esther's hands for ever for five pounds – with results that are not hard to imagine.

'and if you likes to go out again as wet-nurse, I'll take the second off yer 'ands, too, and at the same price.'

In general, though, the line between murder and neglect was difficult to draw. Separating neglect from wilful neglect becomes still more complex when compounded by a background of poverty and ignorance. Nineteenth-century mothers returned to their factories leaving half-starved infants to be quietened with laudanum and treacle by baby-minders. Toddlers who survived were sent out into the streets to 'play':

Some were crushed, some were lost, some caught colds and fevers, crept back into their garret or cellars, were dosed with Godfrey's cordial, and died in peace. (Disraeli, 1845)

Disraeli, inflamed by the investigations revealed in Parliamentary Blue Books as much as by his own observations, decided that

Infanticide is practiced as extensively and legally in England as it is on the banks of the Ganges. . . .

But Engels (1845), writing at the same time, considered that the parents were not to blame; they had done what they could, but that was so little.

These unhappy children, perishing in this terrible way, are victims of our social disorder.

He accused the ruling class of 'social murder'.

Little Looey, whose death in the East End Jago was described in the previous chapter, was certainly a victim of 'social disorder' in Engels' sense. So too, it may be argued, were the Birmingham babies who died so frequently: 'Birmingham is said to be a very healthy town', Mr J. Edward White reported to the Children's Employment Commission in 1864. He sounded a bit doubtful about that, given the overall pollution, the filth he had observed in and around the vast number of small workshops there, and the crowded, ill-lit and airless conditions of the larger factories.

He admitted that housing was better laid-out and the houses themselves less crowded, than in other great manufacturing cities, which might counteract some of the squalor of the surroundings. Still sounding less than convinced, he continued,

The rate of infant mortality, which had attracted the attention of the Medical Officer of the Privy Council, is referred *by him* mainly to the employment of married women in factories, leading to the neglect of their infants. (White, 1864: my italics)

Poverty drove the women back to the factories so early after a birth but, even if they had stayed home with the baby, what could they have done to save their children in such an environment?

Where the neglect was wilful, desperation rather than callous ruthlessness was often the motive. Drawing on his experiences as a medical student in the 1890s, Somerset Maugham described the verminous, filthy one-roomed tenements of London:

The people who dwelt here lived from hand to mouth. Babies were unwelcome, the man received them with surly anger, the mother with despair: it was one more mouth to feed, and there

was little enough wherewith to feed those already there. Philip
often discerned the wish that the child might be born dead or
might die quickly. He delivered one woman of twins (a source of
humour to the facetious) and when she was told she burst into a
long shrill wail of misery. Her mother said outright:

'I don't know how they're going to feed 'em.'

'Maybe the Lord'll see fit to take 'em to 'imself,' said the
midwife.

Philip caught sight of the husband's face as he looked at the
tiny pair lying side by side, and there was a ferocious sullenness
in it which startled him. He felt in the family assembled there a
hideous resentment against those poor atoms who had come into
the world unwished for; and he had a suspicion that if he did not
speak firmly an 'accident' would occur. Accidents occurred often;
mothers 'overlaid' their babies, and perhaps errors of diet were
not always the result of carelessness.

'I shall come every day,' he said. 'I warn you that if anything
happens to them there'll have to be an inquest.'

The father made no reply, but he gave Philip a scowl. There
was murder in his soul.

'Bless their little 'earts,' said the grandmother, 'what should
'appen to them?' (Maugham, 1915)

Whether the parent(s) or minders intended it or not, the babies –
especially illegitimate babies – died.

In 1869, for example, of the 3979 inquest subjects under one year,
1251, or nearly a third, were 'illegitimate or unknown' at a time
when the official return of illegitimate births was 5.8 per cent or
at the most 8.3 per cent on unofficial estimates. Intriguingly the
picture for 1–7 year olds is very different: of the 1905 inquest
subjects, only 193 were 'illegitimate or unknown'; this contrast
applies throughout the 19th century and to observers . . . it suggested that a wilful holocaust of illegitimates after birth was leaving few unwanted ones above twelve months old. (Rose, 1986)

Babies who started their lives under official supervision, whether
it were of Maugham's medical student or the workhouse, were not
necessarily safe in the longer run. Dr Julian Hunter reported that
illegitimate babies were frequently born in the workhouse, where
they would thrive as well as their legitimate fellows; only to be

reported dead shortly after the child and mother had left. He also noted that among the women who worked in contract 'gangs', moving around the country to plant or harvest particular crops, illegitimate babies fared worse – but not much worse – then legitimate ones.

> In the agricultural population it may be roundly stated that of the illegitimates one third die under a year old, of the others one fourth part. (Hunter, 1863)

Doctors, he claimed, seldom bothered much about making a proper diagnosis of the cause of death; almost all of them agreed that the underlying cause was the mother's neglect.

> The degree of criminality attributed to the women varied, from a sympathising excuse for their ignorance to a downright charge of wilful neglect with the hope of death – in fact, infanticide. (Hunter, 1863)

Inadequate laws, and public sympathy for the desperate mothers – a sympathy which came not only from their jury peers but from lawyers, judges and doctors – prevented many cases of infanticide from ever being formally brought, and others from achieving a verdict of guilty. As with abortion, the draconian consequences if a woman were to be found guilty were also a deterrent against such a judgement. If a woman was found to have committed infanticide, the sentence was death. It was generally commuted to life-imprisonment but even so, there was a widespread feeling that the crime did not justify the punishment.

Illegitimacy was a recognised handicap, both to the mother and to the child itself. Those who would do nothing to hasten the baby's end might yet be relieved should it die naturally. Mrs Madhurst, an old village woman, explained her daughter's mourning to a visitor:

> Jenny's child, she said, had died. . . . It was, she felt, better out of the way, even though insurance offices, for reasons she did not pretend to follow, would not willingly insure such stray lives. 'Not but what Jenny didn't tend to Arthur as though he'd come all proper at de end of de first year – like Jenny herself.' Thanks to Miss Florence, the child had been buried with a pomp which, in Mrs Madhurst's opinion, more than covered the small irregularity of its birth. . . . (Kipling, 1908)

Jenny's Arthur had been passionately loved by his mother, and his grandmother clearly did not feel that, at the village level, illegitimacy was as much of a stigma as it might be elsewhere. Nevertheless, the child 'was better out of the way'. Her only regret about his death was that there was no insurance payout; insurance companies, which had come under attack for providing a positive incentive to infanticide (Rose, 1986), were by the end of the century rather more selective in accepting premiums for high-risk cases.

Abortion was the other major alternative for those faced with an unwanted – often illegitimate – pregnancy. Some authorities have doubts about the frequency of abortions in pre-sepsis days, on the grounds that women would have been deterred by the danger of the process (McKeown, 1976). However, the high rates of unsafe abortion in countries like India or Bangladesh today, which result in a high proportion of maternal deaths, suggest that women are prepared to go to considerable lengths to avoid a birth if their situation is sufficiently desperate (Khan et al., 1986).

Colette captured the atmosphere of resigned determination in a story of a pregnant showgirl in the first decade of this century. She and two other colleagues go to visit the girl, and find her dying; her abortionist mother had been, not for the first time, incompetent.

'Old murderess,' muttered Carmen. 'Clumsy old beast.' Neither of them showed any surprise. I saw that they were, both of them, thoroughly aware of and inured to such things. They could contemplate impartially certain risks and certain secret dealing of which I knew nothing. There was a type of criminality which they passively and discreetly acknowledged when confronted with the danger of having a child. They talked of the monstrous in a perfectly matter of fact way. (Colette, 1937)

Women who could afford their services went to midwives and doctors for help, and one investigator in the 1860s concluded that such abortions were 'extremely numerous' (Rose, 1986). Other women presumably used the local network of unqualified practitioners, or attempted to abort themselves.

A major alternative to using instruments in order to achieve abortion – and one which many women may have thought less risky – was to use a drug. Advertisements for abortifacients were by the 1850s well known in England and even in Australia (Siedlecky and Wyndham, 1990). The advertisements were usually for drugs whose ingredients varied from strong laxatives to poisons. Some were effective, if dangerous to the mother as well as fatal to the foetus; others were neither. The large numbers of advertisements and their continuation into the twentieth century suggest that the use of drugs for an abortion was quite widespread.

The most comprehensive record of the use of drugs and other abortifacients, as well as infanticide, was collected in Australia in 1906 as a result of the 1903 Royal Commission on the Decline of the Birth Rate in New South Wales. The commission had heard extensive evidence from police, doctors, pharmacists and others of the use of various techniques to avoid unwanted pregnancy (Hicks, 1978) and so a fuller investigation of their availability was instituted in the form of a Royal Commission on Secret Drugs and Cures (Beale, 1907).

One study (Quiggin, 1988) of the advertising of abortifacients found that initially they were aimed at young girls and older women, designed presumably to meet the needs of those pre-maritally pregnant or those who wanted a respite from childbearing. Towards the end of the century they were addressed to women in general, as though any woman might wish to end a pregnancy.

Even in rural areas there seems to have been widespread recourse to drugs for abortion, as well as some use of instruments. Dr Julian Hunter reported to the Privy Council in 1863 that the areas which employed rural work-gangs of women had large numbers of baby deaths allegedly resulting from premature births. Hunter pointed out that, as by far the greater number of these deaths took place in the summer quarter, it was likely that many resulted from the conditions of women's work in the fields. However, he went on, gang work was notoriously linked to immorality and

is said to account for the high numbers of illegitimate births in the counties involved. Attempts to produce premature births on this account were reported, though they were not known to be very common. A French woman was said to have done a great deal of mischief in this way at Wisbeach; and a notion that the young women have that such drugs as savine or turpentine will induce miscarriages leads them to take large quantities, from which, although they are usually disappointed of their wishes, may be expected a diminished viability of the child. . . . (Hunter, 1863)

Some doctors would pretend to connive with the unfortunate women, hoping to delay their recourse to alternatives until the pregnancy was too far advanced for abortion. Colette, describing her brother's country practice in France in the 1880s, wrote,

Paris and the Latin Quarter had not prepared him for so much amorous knowledge, secrecy and variety. But impudence was not lacking either, at least in the case of the girls who came boldly to his weekly surgery declaring that they had not 'seen' since they got their feet wet two months ago, pulling a drowned hen out of a pond.

'That's fine!' my brother would say, after his examination . . . 'I'm going to give you a prescription.'

He watched for the look of pleasure and contempt and the joyful reddening of the cheek and wrote out the prescription agreed between doctor and chemist: 'Mica panis, two pills to be taken after each meal.' The remedy might avert or, at least, delay, the intervention of 'the woman who knew about herbs.' (Colette, 1937)

In the last quarter of the century, illegitimate fertility was falling fast. By 1901 it had fallen more than twice as much as fertility within marriage. The rapidity of the decline suggests that while more people within and outside marriage were using birth control, and possibly more effective methods, those who wished to avoid an illegitimate child were doing so on a greater scale.

Before the declines in fertility began in the 1870s, the evidence indicates that couples seldom stopped having children at any particular family size. As the mean age of the mothers at the birth of their final child was over 39 years, the evidence also suggests that most were having children more or less until the end of their reproductive lives. Demographers somewhat confusingly call this pattern of childbearing 'natural fertility', by which they mean that couples do not deliberately attempt to limit family size by ceasing to have children while, biologically, they still could do so. In this sense, family limitation was uncommon in England.

That is not quite the same thing as saying that couples did not practice 'birth control', if birth control is defined as any deliberate action to space or prevent births (Knodel, 1978). Given the rather small numbers of children that the English produced over their fertile lives, it seems likely that many of them did practice some form of birth control in the hope of avoiding a pregnancy at a particular time. A couple might wish to avoid a pregnancy if they were not yet married, or to postpone another birth if they had a recent baby.

Breastfeeding was one traditional way of spacing pregnancies, especially if it was combined with sexual abstinence – avoiding the risk of a further pregnancy while the mother's resources were devoted to the new infant. We saw in the previous chapter that Jane Austen recommended 'a simple regimen of separate rooms' for a frequently-pregnant relative. Some argue that during the Victorian period, breastfeeding was general, at least among the urban working classes (Woods *et al.*, 1988/9). An alternative view is that breastfeeding may have declined substantially (Teitelbaum, 1984). Other things being equal, such a decline would have resulted in increases in fertility: that in fact fertility did not increase might indicate that abstinence was an important mechanism for spacing pregnancies.

Abstaining from sexual intercourse for quite lengthy periods may not have been as difficult as some have argued (Knodel and van der Walle, 1986), especially for the poor. Cramped living accommodation, where the whole family might share not just a room but even a bed, was not conducive to spontaneous sexual activity. While there is no evidence that chronic undernourishment produces sterility, the combination of inadequate diet and the exhaustion produced by long hours of heavy work probably led to low rates of intercourse. Couples themselves aged faster when life-expectation was so much shorter. In the poorer parts of the Third World today it is still quite common to meet men and women in their thirties who look fifty at least; many prematurely-aged people would have been found in the industrialised countries a century ago.

Women who were exhausted and often ill as the result of frequent childbearing and poverty might welcome the cessation of sexual relations. All too often, sex was not about shared intimacy and commitment but the husband's demand for 'his rights' and his wife's fear of another pregnancy. One woman, born in 1903 to an out-of-work father and a mother who took in washing, recalled overhearing her parents:

> I heard Mum, say, 'You can put that bloody thing away. I've had enough.' Her says 'I've had a baker's dozen and you ain't having no more.' (Holdsworth, 1988)

The belief that after a certain time a woman had the right to be left alone seems to have been strengthened at a later date, when it was combined with her right to peace after a certain number of children (Ware, 1979).

Among the wealthier couples, convention decreed a separate 'dressing room', containing some sort of bed for the husband; he did not automatically, or invariably, share the official double bed in which his wife slept. When Soames Forsyte finds that Irene has locked their bedroom door, he at first thinks it accidental:

> entering his dressing-room, where the gas was also lit and burning low, he went quickly to the other door. That too was locked. Then he noticed that the camp bed he occasionally used was prepared, and his sleeping-suit laid out upon it. . . . (Galsworthy, 1906)

Sir Henry Harcourt, whose wife has left him and whose finances and ambitions have failed him, determines to kill himself.

> He waited patiently, sitting in his chair for some hour or so; nay, it may have been for two hours, for the house was still, and the servants were in bed. Then, rising from his chair, he turned the lock of his dressing-room door. It was a futile precaution, if it meant anything, for the room had another door, which opened to his wife's chamber. . . . (Trollope, 1859)

Couples who had remained unmarried until their late twenties or their thirties, and who had made prudent rather than ardent matches, were not necessarily averse to shorter or longer periods of abstinence.

For those who did not wish to give up sexual intercourse, an alternative way of avoiding a pregnancy was withdrawal, or *coitus interruptus*, helpfully explained in the Old Testament for any schoolboy. Onan, having been told, as was customary, to marry his dead brother's widow, avoided giving her a child:

> he spilled the seed upon the ground lest he should give seed to his brother. (Genesis, 38:9)

There is a nice reference to the use of withdrawal in the bastardy cases of colonial Pennsylvania. A young man accused of getting a girl with child admitted,

'I f—d her once, but I minded my pullbacks. I sware I did not get it' (Wells, 1980)

Minding one's pullbacks may have been more popular among those – like this young man – who wanted to escape an illegitimate pregnancy, rather than among married couples. The problem is that we do not really know. Some modern authors (Knodel and van der Walle, 1986) doubt that withdrawal was widely acceptable or even known before the onset of the fertility transition; others (Woods, 1987) believe it to have been popular. In 1854 Dr Drysdale claimed that withdrawal was 'very frequently practised by married and unmarried men'. Drysdale himself was not an advocate for withdrawal: he was trying to promote the use of the sponge.

Both abstinence and withdrawal have the advantage – for their users – that they involve no equipment or outside assistance; they are behaviours which can – and did – remain entirely private. Because they were private and intimate, they are seldom mentioned in writing. Mary Noel may have been referring to withdrawal when she talked about 'proper measures' being taken to prevent another pregnancy for her niece; equally, she may not. Because such methods involved neither goods nor services we cannot track down their use through advertisements or other sources.

The first published discussions of birth control in England are believed to have been those of Francis Place in 1822 and 1823; the latter year saw his three *Handbills*, the first of which was addressed to 'The Married of Both Sexes'. The others targeted specific classes among those married couples. While the more general text mentioned both *coitus interruptus* and the sponge, the other two described only the sponge, a piece 'the size of a green walnut' attached to a narrow ribbon. He claimed it was a method which had existed for some time but had only become popular in the previous two years, as the result of 'a more extensive knowledge of the process'.

Place, an ex-tailor and political activist, had a sophisticated talent for marketing. One version of his *Handbill* was designed for those 'in Genteel Life'; the other for 'working people'. The first concentrates the argument for use of the sponge on maternal ill-health – the 'sufferings of the married woman' – before pointing out that

In the middle ranks, the most virtuous and praiseworthy efforts are perpetually made to keep up the respectability of the family; but a continual increase of children gradually yet certainly renders every effort to prevent degradation unavailing, it paralizes by rendering helpless all exertion, and the family sinks into poverty and despair.

The appeal in the other *Handbill* could have been taken from Ricardo's economic theory. Place reminds the workers that when there are too many applicants for work,

wages are reduced very low and the working people become little better than slaves.

When wages have thus been reduced to a very small sum, working people can no longer maintain their children as all good and respectable people wish to maintain their children, but are compelled to neglect them;– to send them to different employ-ments;– to Mills and Manufactories, at a very early age.

The misery of these poor children. . . .

These appeals – to the middle-classes' fear of slipping down the social scale, and to the working classes' dread of low or no wages and desire for a better future for their children – were, it is thought, widely circulated.

They were followed in 1825 by a book, *Every Woman's Book; or What is Love?* published by Richard Carlile. Carlile was another radical who had been a journeyman tinman; he was also a friend of Place, whose advertising abilities may have suggested the title.

A number of other publications followed, some of which ran into several editions and were, presumably, quite widely read (Himes, 1936). A (male) Yorkshire textile worker in 1832 told a Parliamen-tary committee that

there are certain books which have gone forth to inform depraved persons of a way in which they may indulge their corrupt pas-sions and still avoid having illegitimate children. (Rowbotham, 1973)

Nicholas Higgins, Mrs Gaskell's (1855) Manchester weaver, seems to have produced only two daughters before his wife's death when the older child was around 10 or 12 years of age. He is contemptu-ous of his neighbour, the 'poor good-for-nought' Bourcher with his feckless and sickly wife, and eight children under the age of nine. Nicholas's political views suggest that he was likely to be familiar with at least some of the works of Place and Carlile; it is not impos-sible to imagine him as an early user of contraception.

From the 1850s at least, publications on contraception included descriptions of the douche and condoms as well. Credit for the invention of the douche was claimed by Charles Knowlton, an American. His book *Fruits of Philosophy: or, the private companion of young married couples* (1832) argued that douching had the great advantage of putting control of fertility into the hands of the woman. It is estimated to have sold about a thousand copies a year in Britain until the 1870s, when the figures shot up exponentially to reach, eventually, 350 000 (Teitelbaum, 1984).

Condoms had been available since at least the eighteenth century but, being made of sheepgut, they were expensive. Nevertheless, their contribution to mankind was quickly recognised, with Joseph Gay (1716) extolling

The New Machine a sure Defense shall prove,
And guard the sex against the Harm of Love

and another, anonymous, poet even writing a *Panegyrick upon Cundums*. This states how condoms permitted

Joys untasted but for them
Unknown Big Belly and the Squalling Brat.
(Finch and Green, 1963)

However, even when the invention of vulcanised rubber led to their mass production in the 1880s, condoms are estimated to have cost from two to ten shillings a dozen, which put them out of reach of the poor.

Drysdale, whose solid book *Elements of Social Science* (1854) was successful to the tune of 35 English editions and 10 European translations, claimed that condoms were widely used, though more on the Continent than in England. He was unenthusiastic about withdrawal:

physically injurious and is apt to produce nervous disorder and sexual enfeeblement and congestion, from the sudden interruption it gives to the venereal act, whose pleasures moreover, it interferes with.

The condom was no better:

dulls the enjoyment and frequently produces impotence in the man and disgust in both parties, so that it also is injurious.

Use of the sponge, on the other hand, could be 'done by the woman' and was therefore recommended.

Any preventive means, to be satisfactory, must be used by the *woman*, as it spoils the passion and impulsiveness of the venereal act, if a man has to think of them.

Lack of enthusiasm on the part of men about male methods easily led, when contraception became more widespread, to a demand that the woman take entire responsibility for birth control. Mildred, in *Of Human Bondage*, was dropped by her lover after a fight:

He was frightened because I told him a baby was coming. I kept it from him as long as I could. Then I had to tell him. He said it was my fault and I ought to have known better. (Maugham, 1915)

The book is set in the 1890s; by that time Mildred could, in addition to the douche and sponge, have chosen pessaries as a form of protection. Developed by a chemist, Walter John Rendell, and first commercially manufactured in 1886, pessaries had achieved worldwide sales by the end of the century, partly as a result of the enthusiastic endorsement of Annie Besant (Finch and Green, 1963). She could also have considered what in English was known as a 'Dutch Cap' after W. P. J. Mensinga. He had popularised the technique which – like the condom – depended on the invention of vulcanised rubber to become readily available (Teitelbaum, 1984).

A major impediment to those considering the possibility of contraceptive use must have been the extraordinarily partisan advice which was given about individual methods by various authors. Robert Dale Owen, an American whose book *Moral Physiology: or, a brief and plain treatise on the population question* went through many editions after its publication in England in 1832, disapproved sponge and condom and recommended withdrawal; Knowlton was an enthusiast for the sponge alone; Albutt in *The Wives Handbook* (1884 or 1885), on the other hand, recommended diaphragms and condoms; while Annie Besant in the *Law of Population* (1879) gave only qualified approval to douche and condom, queried the safe period, but supported withdrawal and (in later editions) pessaries and caps. Conflicting advice, and the dire warnings of the 'injurious' effects of the various methods disliked by the authors, surely discouraged many in England then, as today they do in the Third World.

In 1876, Annie Besant and Charles Bradlaugh, hearing of the imprisonment of a publisher for reissuing a version of Knowlton's pamphlet, determined to publish it themselves as a test case. The case resulted in immense publicity and the press coverage brought the subject of birth control into current affairs as well as into people's homes. The impact of such publicity seems to have been at least as important as the fact that they finally won their case: the circulation of all existing books and leaflets on contraception increased dramatically. Together with Besant's own book and Albutt's, it is estimated that at least a million copies of the various publications were sold between 1876 and 1891.

The Besant–Bradlaugh success at law may have helped to overcome two other barriers to contraceptive acceptance. The first was that contraception was seen as 'unnatural', against the natural, proper and God-given order of things. Drysdale, among others, recognised this perception and attempted to minimise its impact:

but sexual abstinence is infinitely more unnatural; in fact it is so unnatural, and therefore sinful, that it is totally incompatible with health and happiness, and produces the most widespread and desolating diseases. It is granted that preventive intercourse is unnatural, but the circumstances of our lives leave us no alternative. If we were to obey all the natural impulses, and follow our sexual desires like the inferior animals, which lead a natural life, we should be forced to prey upon and check the growth of each other, just as they do. . . . (Drysdale, *op. cit.*)

The second barrier was that the most urgent need for contraception came – as it had always come – from those in illicit relationships. Condoms in particular had long been used as a preventive against venereal disease.

I picked up a girl in the Strand; went into a court with intention to enjoy her in Armour. But she had none. (Boswell, 1782)

The association with immorality was what put Malthus off contraception and made him prescribe late marriage or celibacy as the only acceptable means of population limitation.

The remaining checks of the preventive kind are: the sort of intercourse which renders some of the women of large towns unprolific; a general corruption of morals with regard to the sex, which has a similar effect; unnatural passions and improper arts to prevent the consequences of irregular connections. These evidently come under the head of vice. (Malthus, 1830)

Thus the Besant–Bradlaugh publication of a contraceptive treatise had been described in the indictment as being designed to corrupt morals, especially the morals of the young, and to

incite and encourage the said subjects to indecent, obscene, unnatural and immoral practices. . . . (Teitelbaum, 1984)

Winning the case implied contraceptives were not indecent, obscene, unnatural and immoral – and neither was their use by married couples. The significance of the case may have been less that it made people aware of contraception, than that it cloaked contraception in a new respectability.

The cloak of respectability was needed from another perspective, too. Early English advocates of birth control came from the radical working-class Left. Place had campaigned against the Combination Laws designed to prevent strikes. Carlile edited a paper called *The Republican*. Even Drysdale, a doctor whose father was Sir William, City Treasurer of Edinburgh, suggested that contraception would make free love possible, and that by its judicious use all those superfluous women could have 'a due share of the pleasures of Love, and also the blessings of motherhood' (Drysdale, *op. cit.*) – to the tune of two or three children apiece!

The middle classes were unlikely to look kindly on such advocates; neither were the more conservative sections of the working class. When the contraceptive revolution did come, it was initiated by the middle classes (Banks, 1954) and – if evidence from a study of Sheffield has wider application – especially the lower middle classes. The clerks, schoolteachers, shopowners and assistants of Sheffield sound exactly like the 'genteel' for whom Place wrote: people on the fringes of the solid middle class, who could so easily lose their status as a result of the expense of a large family. But they were much more likely to listen to a judge than to Francis Place. So too were the more conservative or 'respectable' sections of the working class, sections of which seem to have been as quick – or almost as quick – to use contraception (Woods, 1987).

9

Conclusions

Man had entered the Nineteenth century using only his own and animal power, supplemented by that of wind and water, much as he had entered the Thirteenth, or, for that matter, the First. He entered the Twentieth with his capacities in transportation, communication, production, manufacture and weaponry multiplied a thousandfold by the energy of machines. Industrial society gave man new powers and new scope while at the same time building up new pressures in prosperity and poverty, in growth of population and crowding in cities, in antagonism of classes and groups, in separation from nature and from satisfaction in individual work. Science gave man new welfare and new horizons while it took away belief in God and certainty in a scheme of things he knew. By the time he left the Nineteenth century he had as much new unease as ease. (Tuchman, 1966)

The turmoil of this extraordinary century, the pace and extent of change which marked it, are difficult even to imagine. To understand fully what it was like for people living at the time, let alone to trace all the influences which affected them, is clearly impossible. At the very most, by using every technique of historical research, we may be able to formulate a partial picture: one that appears to present some sort of a likeness and which contains a fair amount of what Poo Bah called

> corroborative detail, intended to give artistic verisimilitude to an otherwise bald and unconvincing narrative. (Gilbert, 1885)

It is some of the detail around the bald fact of a change in family size which this book has tried to explore. In doing so, it has been limited in two ways: by the selection of authors, and what those authors choose to tell us. Today, a study of marriage, fertility and families would be carefully designed to answer specific questions about attitudes and behaviour; the questionnaire would be pre-tested to ensure that respondents could understand the questions and would answer them; it would be administered to a statistically representative cross-sectional sample of the population. In this book, on the other hand, we have to get what we can from words written in quite another context, by highly individual people, about thoughts and situations which were 'typical' only in the sense that their audiences believed them to reflect some sort of reality.

Somewhat to my surprise, the voices do seem very often to be acting in chorus, telling us similar stories and revealing similar attitudes. When they do, I think we are entitled to accept that they do encapsulate some sort of common – though not necessarily universal – experience.

I think, too, that the details these writers provide, and the way they write about them, give us an insight into the way people lived and thought. Squire Brown taking the best boys out of the village school to amuse his young son Tom, and the comfortable way in which Hughes describes him doing so, surely says something about the perceived value of education for the poor in the mid-century, as well as about the relations between rural landowners and their dependants or employees.

Mrs Pooter playing her cottage piano, bought 'on the three years' system' of hire purchase brings to life the genteel aspirations of the ever-growing lower middle class, as well as the economics of achieving those aspirations.

The design of a modern survey is usually based on a theoretical framework of some sort. Given that one cannot ask every possible question, assumptions have to be made about the areas of questioning which may be most productive, and why. In collecting material for this book, I could make no such assumptions. I did not know what I might find; I simply had to take what was given me, and try to see whether there were any consistent themes emerging.

The key one, I think, is that both the voices of the past, and demographic reconstructions, indicate that the British never saw very large families as particularly desirable. Something under six children had been the typical number produced by couples as far into the past as we can go; and many couples would lose at least one at some stage during its childhood. The comments of our authors suggest that, at least from the beginning of the nineteenth century, those who had substantially more children than was typical were seen as comic, inept, or sad victims of fate.

How many children made 'too many' seems to have been invariably linked with how many a couple could provide for. Whether it is Jane Austen, talking of Mrs Price having 'such a superfluity of children, and such a want of almost everything else'; or Hardy's yokels sagely observing that 'Where the pigs be many, the wash runs thin', the theme is one of reproduction outstripping resources.

This, I would suggest, makes it difficult to argue, as some have done, that the question of preferred family size simply did not arise before the advent of fertility decline. It seems to me more reasonable to assume that while many, or even most, people went on having children throughout their fertile lives, many regulated the potential numbers either by delaying marriage until they were in a position to support those who might eventuate, or by trying to space the number of babies they produced. Without alternative contraception, abstinence for the rest of one's life may have been an unattractive option for many, but abstinence for a time acceptable to more. Especially so when a new baby required time and attention and the wife was breastfeeding.

This is not to say that everybody was consciously practising 'birth control'. Many, as we have seen, appear to have had larger families than they were happy about, and have accepted the fact with gloomy fatalism. Others may well have chosen to delay marriage until they could support a family, without ever doing an exact calculation about the precise number of children which might be produced in the remaining fertile years. Yet others may have tried to ensure a well-spaced family primarily to safeguard the health of mother and child. All the same, on some level they were making choices, and these choices were eventually reflected in family size.

And if that is so, then the question about the nineteenth century fertility decline is not 'What gave people the idea that controlling fertility was possible and desirable?' but 'What made people decide that a smaller number of births than five or six would be preferable?'

Admittedly, a preference for three or four children would require far more conscious intervention than had been required for the five or six. Spacing or avoiding births would have to be a matter for deliberate and rigorous effort. Some methods to enable people to space or avoid pregnancies had been around throughout the century. For effective birth control, however, more widespread use had to be made of them. Given the limitations of both abstinence and *coitus interruptus*, it was probably also necessary to have other reliable and acceptable methods available. In other words, before people could make the decision about smaller families, they had to know that the means to implement those choices were available.

Demographic statistics which show a fall in family size are the aggregates of the outcome of decisions by individual families. In fiction as well as in fact, we have seen that the Victorian family was far from the stable monolith which later generations often pictured. If anything, families were more like an amoeba, expanding and contracting with new alliances and frequent deaths, absorbing new step-relatives and losing other family members through migration or social mobility.

The uncertainties of family life, and even of family existence, led, as I have suggested, to a psychic fluidity in thinking about the family: a willingness to accept missing heirs, secret marriages, and long-lost relatives as routine ingredients in a novelist's plot. Such ingredients suggest a fundamental unease about the boundaries of the family and one's ability to order or preserve those boundaries against arbitrary fates.

Perhaps the ideal family – solid, prosperous and enduring – gained the status of myth because the Victorians themselves so much wanted to believe in it, and themselves to be a part of the stability which it implied. In a rapidly-altering world, it would have been something to cling on to.

Family instability during the nineteenth century was much exacerbated by social mobility, which was an element in, as well as a consequence of, the great upheavals of the century. It was far from uni-directional; a family like Mrs Gaskell's Thorntons, or Charles Dickens's parents, could plummet to unimaginable – by today's standards – destitution almost as easily as an almost illiterate ropemaker like William Lovett could become a leading member of the new industrial proletariat, or a teacher raise her whole family to the middle classes. Money and social class, acquired or lost, are constant preoccupations of the Victorian novel.

For most of the period, and particularly during the early part of the century, there were more winners than losers: Britain led the Industrial Revolution and, despite the frequent slumps, there seems to have been an overall optimism, a delight in progress and innovation, which suggested that the future could be met with confidence. The 'marvel of England's greatness' could be taken for granted. The sense of constant overall material expansion to meet increasing demand may have encouraged couples to go on producing comparatively large families.

By the 1850s, however, most of Europe had industrialised too, together with the New World: increasing foreign competition and the Depression which began in 1876 and continued throughout the final quarter of the century would have undermined any such confidence. Galsworthy, pondering on the declining birth rate, wrote,

A student of statistics must have noticed that the birth rate had varied in accordance with the rate of interest for your money. Grandfather 'Superior Dosset' Forsyte in the early nineteenth century had been getting ten per cent for his, hence ten children. Those ten, leaving out the four who had not married, and Juley, whose husband Septimus Small had, of course, died almost at once, had averaged from four to five per cent of theirs, and produced accordingly. The twenty-one whom they produced were now getting barely three per cent in the Consuls to which their fathers had mostly tied the Settlements they made to avoid death duties, and the six of them who had been reproduced had seventeen children, or just the proper two and five-sixths per person.

By the last quarter of the century, many of the prosperous middle classes had established themselves for two or three generations, just as Galsworthy's Forsytes had done. 'Clogs to clogs in three generations' goes the old Yorkshire proverb, and Galsworthy too suspected that the very success of the earlier Forsytes had undermined initiative and daring in their descendants.

A distrust of their earning powers, natural where a sufficiency is guaranteed, together with the knowledge their fathers did not die, kept them cautious. If one had children and not much income, the standard of taste and comfort must of necessity go down; what was enough for two was not enough for four, and so on – it would be better to wait and see what Father did.

With social mobility went physical mobility: the removal to new towns or suburbs where neighbours and workmates, rather than the extended family, provided support, and peer pressure replaced that of the traditional establishment. Nicholas Higgins and his neighbours take care of the children of the weaver who has killed himself; the weaver kills himself because he is a strike-breaker who cannot endure the hostility of his fellows. The Pooters live up to the expectations of their friends, not those of Mrs Pooter's annually-visited mama.

Newspapers and books were shared between friends or fellow

workers, at home or in the social and political clubs that sprang up across the country. The discussions which took place were seen by their more conservative contemporaries as profoundly threatening; the tone in which they wrote about the debates of the 'Uninformed' leave little doubt of that. (I was sharply reminded of the tone in which Europeans described the activities of newly-educated Africans, in my colonial childhood.) The newspapers and books these working and lower middle classes read, and the ideas they talked about, fed on and fuelled demands for greater democracy – for the right of everybody to be involved in decision-making.

Among the topics which came up, contraception seems very likely to have been included, given its links with the radical working-class movement. In the long run, this may have helped create the climate through which smaller families became so swiftly accepted across social classes in Britain. In other European countries, the dissemination was considerably slower.

In the short term, however, the association between fertility control and radicalism may have put off many potential users. They may also have been deterred by the conflicting advice given by the various enthusiasts for family limitation, and their dire warnings about the potential harm of any method other than the one they preferred.

Besides, the methods themselves, until late in the century, remained remarkably old-fashioned in an age which was thrilled by novelty and technological development. Abstinence and *coitus interruptus* and the humble sponge can have had little more glamour than, in the 1970s, the condom had to young men of a post-Pill generation.

The social mobility which was such an outstanding feature of the nineteenth century was both created by education, and encouraged further demands for it. The evidence collected here about the kinds of education which people received – at any level of society – does not suggest that what was directly taught could have been a catalyst for change.

The wealthy continued to get a classical foundation. This was helpful neither in understanding the practicalities of the Industrial Revolution – a steam turbine or the physics of stress – nor in grappling with Darwinism or the literal truth of the Scriptures. Girls got little more than a smattering of 'accomplishments'. The poor learned hardly anything but to read and write – if they were lucky.

But we have had hints that going to school undermined old beliefs and superstitions, and that it set a distance between the older, illiterate, generation and their literate children, leaving parents possibly reluctant to press their views upon a child who was 'a great deal beyond me in learning now', as Susan's mother reported her.

It has also been suggested that learning to read was enough to give those who wanted it access to whole new worlds. Those new worlds in themselves encouraged exploration, so that mechanics like Joe Scott were forced to think – 'when I see an effect, I look straight for a cause . . .'; and turned young men like Lydgate into doctors ambitious of making 'a link in the chain of discovery'.

Those who encouraged education among the poor did so to correct the moral values of inadequately-raised children. Indirectly and indeed in opposition to their stated aim, they let loose an explosive force for change. Its increasing desirability meant people wanted more and more of it; the costs of a child included ever-longer periods of schooling.

The intellectual ferment of the period was accessible to anybody who could read or persuade somebody to read to him. Among its many manifestations, it encouraged others to accept, with Queen Victoria, that childbirth should not necessarily involve suffering just because the Bible said it did. If suffering were, like the cholera, no longer 'jidgment, Sir, a jidgment of God' then women had the right to express their fears of dying in childbirth, or becoming worn out and sickly by repeated pregnancies. The health benefits of family planning to the 'suffering of a married woman', stressed by Francis Place, seem to have become widely recognised as the century progressed.

In addition, the right of women to control their own affairs and their bodies was gradually and reluctantly being recognised, in law as well as in literature. An unhappy marriage could (admittedly with difficulty) be ended; a married woman could independently manage her financial affairs. To a great extent, personal autonomy seems to have been the only right which society was willing to grant women; as we have seen, on the wider issues of the franchise or careers Victorian writers were silent, and so presumably were many of their readers.

Even this single right to limited autonomy was granted only to married women. Single women remained 'the girls at home', trapped in the frenzy of despair whose scream echoes across the accounts we have heard. That male pillar of Victorian virtues, Trollope, as well as the remote and cosmopolitan Henry James, reported the cry as accurately and as sympathetically as did the women writers: it was obviously a phenomenon none could escape. It indicated a desperation made worse by the fact that, for many women, single dependence was an endless prospect. Not all of those single women could marry; even if they did, a prudent match and inadequate outlets for their wish 'to be doing something' might leave them still profoundly unsatisfied.

It seems to me that some married women at least, having been 'the girl at home' for many years and knowing only too well the dreary prospects for those who did not marry, might wish to limit the number of daughters they had. The problem of 'superfluous women' was widely discussed: who would happily add to their number?

To allow married women the right to a say in the number of children they bore might have been a logical outcome of extending them the right of personal autonomy. Handing over, or at least sharing, decisions about family size might also have lessened the guilt of men who understood perfectly well that women were unhappy, but who could imagine no societally-acceptable solution to their fundamental problems. 'Natural law' had reinforced old prejudices.

One difficulty in bringing questions of family size into the home was the cult of female purity. Those men – and they were probably many – who associated birth control with prostitution and immorality would have been reluctant to suggest the use of similar techniques to their wives. The expanding range of female methods – sponge, douche, cap and spermicides, to say nothing of all those advertisements for drugs to 'regulate the system' – offered a different selection of choices; one which perhaps was distanced from the improper connotations of the condom. By delineating contraception as 'women's business', a man could simultaneously offer her further autonomy, while making sure that it was her fault if anything went wrong. 'He said it was my fault and I ought to have known better', said Somerset Maugham's poor Mildred.

Not all women, of course, were unhappy and frustrated. For the Clarrie Pooters, their comfortable little homes, decorated with a new profusion of consumer goods, in which they could be 'professional' housewives, were probably immensely desirable. Such homes and circumstances marked a standard of living and a status unknown to their parents or grandparents.

As the responsibility for bringing up children became ever more significant, the role of the housewife further expanded. But so too did the demands made upon housewives: demands for a standard of care of house and children which were not easy to achieve with limited assistance. Clarrie had only one maid-of-all-work; Nancy Tarrant the additional support of the old family housekeeper. Yet, as we heard, she found that raising even one child properly involved an exhausting twelve-hour day. Children not only stretched the budget; their calls for time and attention, in late Victorian England which had boosted their importance, became more difficult to meet with every addition to the family. And not mothers alone, but fathers too, were increasingly subject to the demands of their children, for companionship as well as cash.

Throughout the nineteenth century, it seems that there were conflicting pressures influencing people in their decisions about children and family limitation. Some influences such as optimism, rising living standards and the equivocal status of contraception, probably encouraged the *status quo*. Others, including the greater importance and demands of children, the enhanced autonomy (though not status) of women, and the influence of science and secularisation on social values, helped towards a reappraisal of family size. From the 1870s on, the balance between the gains from, and the opportunity costs of, larger families shifted decisively. In doing so, the shift brought other consequences. Fewer pregnancies, as well as the greater attention paid to those children who were born, helped to produce the first significant declines in infant mortality and intensified the falls in child deaths. The demographic transition to low birth and death rates – that unique achievement of today's world – had begun.

Bibliography

Where a text has been directly quoted, the edition I have used is also indicated, if that is not the original one.

Abram, W. A. (1868), 'Social Conditions and Political Prospects of the Lancashire Workmen', in Pike, *qv*.

Albutt, H. A. (1884 or 1885), *The Wives Handbook*.

Anderson, Michael and Morse, Donald J. (1993), 'High Fertility, High Emigration, Low Nuptiality: Adjustment Processes in Scotland's Demographic Experience, 1861–1914', Parts I and II, *Population Studies* 47 (1 and 2).

Austen, Jane (1811), *Sense and Sensibility*, J. M. Dent, London, 1963.

—— (1814), *Mansfield Park*, J. M. Dent, London, 1950.

—— (1816), *Emma*, World's Classics, Oxford, 1960.

—— (1818), *Persuasion*, Doubleday, New York, n.d.

Bamford, Samuel (1844), *Passages in the Life of a Radical*, MacGibbon and Kee, London, 1967.

Banks, J. A. (1954), *Prosperity and Parenthood*, Routledge and Kegan Paul, London.

—— and Banks, Olive (1964), *Feminism and Family Planning in Victorian England*, Liverpool University Press, Liverpool.

Barker, Theo and Drake, Michael (1982), *Population and Society in Britain, 1850–1980*, Batsford Academic, London.

Barrie, J. M. (1904), *Peter Pan*.

Beale, O. C. (1907), *Report of the Royal Commission on Secret Drugs and Cures*, Commonwealth of Australia Parliamentary Papers, XIX (IV).

Bell, E. Moberly (1942), *Octavia Hill*, Constable, London.

Belloc, Hilaire (1907), *Cautionary Tales; The Penguin Book of Comic and Curious Verse*, Penguin Books, Middlesex, 1961.

Besant, Annie (1879), *The Law of Population*.

Blanch, Lesley (1954), *The Wilder Shores of Love*, Murray, London.

Blythe, Ronald (1969), *Akenfield*, Allen Lane, Penguin Press, Middlesex.

Boldrewood, Rolf (1888), *Robbery Under Arms*, Rigby, Melbourne, 1981.

Booth, General William (1890), *In Darkest England, and the Way Out*, London.

Boswell, James (1782), *London Journal*, in Finch and Green, *qv*.

Brontë, Anne (1847), *Agnes Grey*, J. M. Dent, London, 1963.

Brontë, Charlotte (1847), *Jane Eyre*, Penguin Books, Middlesex, 1959.

—— (1849), *Shirley*, Thomas Nelson, London, n.d.

Brontë, Emily (1847), *Wuthering Heights*.

Buckle, H. T. (1861), *History of Civilisation in England*, in Pike, *qv*.

Burnett, Frances Hodgson (1911), *The Secret Garden*, Heinemann, London, 1921.

Butler, Samuel (1903), *Ernest Pontifex or The Way of All Flesh*, Methuen, London, 1965.
Caldwell, John C. (1976), 'Towards a Restatement of Demographic Theory', *Population and Development Review* 2 (3–4).
Carlile, Richard (1925), *Every Woman's Book: or, What is Love?*.
Carroll, Lewis (1865), *Alice in Wonderland*.
Cecil, David (1978), *A Portrait of Jane Austen*, Book Club Associates, London.
Chadwick, Owen (1975), *The Secularization of the European Mind in the 19th Century*, Cambridge University Press, Cambridge, 1990.
Coale, Ansley J. and Watkins, Susan Cotts (eds) (1986), *The Decline of Fertility in Europe*, Princeton University Press, Princeton, NJ.
Colette (1937), 'Gribiche', *The Stories of Colette*, Mercury Books, London, 1962.
—— (1937), 'The Patriarch', *The Stories of Colette*, Mercury Books, London, 1962.
Collins, William Wilkie (1862), *No Name*, World's Classics, Oxford, 1986.
Corsini, Carlo A. (1977), 'Self-regulating mechanisms of traditional populations before the demographic revolution: European civilisation', *International Population Conference, Mexico*, International Union for the Scientific Study of Population, Ordina Press, Liège.
Dickens, Charles (1837), *The Pickwick Papers*.
—— (1838), *Oliver Twist*.
—— (1839), *Nicholas Nickleby*, J. M. Dent, London, 1970.
—— (1841), *The Old Curiosity Shop*, Oxford University Press, London, 1951.
—— (1843), *A Christmas Carol*.
—— (1848), *Dombey and Son*, Oxford University Press, London, 1957.
—— (1850), *David Copperfield*.
—— (1861), *Great Expectations*.
Disraeli, Benjamin (1845), *Sybil, or The Two Nations*, World's Classics, Oxford, 1981.
Drysdale, George (1854), *The Elements of Social Science*, in Pike, qv.
Edinburgh Review (1862), in Pike, qv.
Eliot, George (1860), *The Mill on the Floss*.
—— (1861), *Silas Marner*.
—— (1872), *Middlemarch*, Penguin Books, Middlesex, 1965.
Elwin, Malcolm (1967), *The Noels and the Milbankes*, Macdonald, London.
Engels, Frederick (1845), *The Condition of the Working Class in England*, Panther Books, St Albans, 1976.
Farrell, M. J. (Molly Keane) (1937), *The Rising Tide*, Virago Modern Classics, London, 1984.
Fielding, Henry (1749), *Tom Jones*, Penguin Books, Middlesex, 1966.
Finch, B. E. and Green, Hugh (1963), *Contraception Through the Ages*, Peter Owen, London.
Flaubert, Gustave (1857), *Madame Bovary*, Penguin Books, Middlesex, 1961.
Ford, Ford Madox (1911), 'Ancient Lights', *Memories and Impressions*, Penguin Books, Middlesex, 1979.
—— (1931), 'Return to Yesterday', ibid.
—— (1938), 'Mightier than the Sword', ibid.
Frayling, Christopher (1972), *Napoleon Wrote Fiction*, Compton Press, Salisbury.

Frederici, Nora, Mason, Karen Oppenheim and Sogner, Solvi (1993), *Women's Position and Demographic Change*, Clarendon Press, Oxford.

Galsworthy, John (1906), *The Man of Property*, Penguin Books/Heinemann, Middlesex, 1970.

—— (1920), *In Chancery*, Penguin Books, Middlesex, 1969.

Gaskell, Mrs (1855), *North and South*, Penguin Books, Middlesex, 1970.

—— (1864–66), *Wives and Daughters*, Penguin Books, Middlesex, 1969.

Gay, Joseph (1716), *The Petticoat*, in Finch and Green, *qv.*

Gerin, Winifred (1967), *Charlotte Brontë: The Evolution of Genius*, Clarendon Press, Oxford.

Gilbert, W. S. (1881), *Patience*, Savoy Operas.

—— (1885), *The Mikado*, Savoy Operas.

Gissing, George (1891), *New Grub Street*, Penguin Books, Middlesex, 1968.

—— (1894), *In the Year of Jubilee*, Hogarth Press, London, 1987.

Glass, D. V. and Eversley, D. E. C. (1965), *Population in History: Essays in Historical Demography*, Edward Arnold, London.

Glass, D. V. (1973), *Numbering the People*, Saxon House, Farnborough.

Grossmith, George and Weedon (1892), *The Diary of a Nobody*, Penguin Books, Middlesex, 1965.

Hair, P. E. H. (1982), 'Children in society 1850–1980', in Barker and Drake, *qv.*

Hajnal, John (1965), 'European Marriage Patterns in Perspective', in Glass and Eversley, *qv.*

Hardy, Thomas (1878), *The Return of the Native*, Penguin Books, Middlesex, 1978.

—— (1886), *The Mayor of Casterbridge*, Pan Books, London, 1978.

Hartley, L. P. (1953), *The Go-Between*, Penguin Books, Middlesex, 1967.

Hibbert, Christopher (1967), *The Making of Charles Dickens*, Longmans Green, London.

Hicks, Neville (1978), *This Sin and Scandal: Australia's Population Debate 1891–1911*, Australian National University Press, Canberra.

Hill, Caroline Southwood (n.d.) in Bell, 1942, *qv.*

Hill, Draper (1965), *Mr Gillray the Caricaturist*, Phaidon Press, London.

Himes, Norman (1936), *Medical History of Contraception*, Schocken, New York, 1970.

Hobcraft, J. Macdonald, J. and Rutstein, S. (1983) 'Child Spacing and Effects on Infant and Child Mortality', *Population Index* 49 (4).

Hobsbawm, E. J. (1962), *The Age of Revolution: 1789–1848*, New American Library, New York, 1964.

Hodge, Jane Aitken (1972), *The Double Life of Jane Austen*, Hodder and Stoughton, London.

Holdsworth, Angela (1988), *Out of the Doll's House: The story of women in the twentieth century*, BBC Books, London.

Howard, Daniel F. (1965), in Butler, *qv.*

Hughes, Thomas (1857), *Tom Brown's Schooldays*, Thomas Nelson, London n.d.

Hunter, Dr Julian (1863), 'Report on the Excessive Mortality of Infants in some Rural Districts of England', in Pike, *qv.*

James, Henry (1881), *The Portrait of a Lady*.

—— (1886), *The Princess Casamassima*, Penguin Books, Middlesex, 1977.

—— (1899), *The Awkward Age*, Penguin Books, Middlesex, 1966.

Kane, Penny (1991), *Women's Health: From womb to tomb*, Macmillan, London.

Kendall, Paul Murray (1962), *The Yorkist Age*, George Allen and Unwin, London.

Khan, Atiqur Rahman, Jahan, Farida Akhter and Begum, S. Firoza (1986), 'Maternal Mortality in Rural Bangladesh: the Jamalpur District', *Studies in Family Planning* 17 (1).

Kingsley, Charles (1857), *Two Years Ago*, Ward Lock, London.

Kingston, R. (1991), 'Suicide in Pregnancy and the Puerperium', *British Medical Journal*, Vol. 302, 19 January.

Kipling, Rudyard (1893), 'The Record of Badalia Heronsfoot', *Many Inventions*, Macmillan, London, 1925.

—— (1894), *The Jungle Book*.

—— (1898), 'The Bridge Builders', *The Day's Work*, Macmillan, London, 1923.

—— (1898), 'William the Conqueror', ibid.

—— (1899), *Stalky and Co.*, Macmillan, London, 1924.

—— (1890), *The Light That Failed*, Macmillan, London, 1927.

—— (1907), 'Baa Baa Black Sheep', *Wee Willie Winkie*, Macmillan, 1916.

—— (1908), 'They', *Traffics and Discoveries*, Macmillan, 1925.

—— (1926), 'The Eye of Allah', *Debits and Credits*, Macmillan, London, 1927.

Kitson Clark, G. (1962), *The Making of Victorian England*, Methuen, London.

Knodel, John (1978), 'Natural Fertility in Pre-industrial Germany', *Population Studies* 32 (3).

Knodel, John and van der Walle (1986), 'Lessons from the Past: Policy implications of Historical Fertility Studies', in Coale and Watkins, *qv*.

Knowlton, Charles (1832), *Fruits of Philosophy: or, The private companion of young married couples*.

Laslett, Peter and Wall, Richard (eds) (1972), *Household and Family in Past Time* , Cambridge University Press, Cambridge.

—— and Oosterveen, Karal and Smith, Richard M. (eds) (1980), *Bastardy and its Comparative History*, Harvard University Press, Cambridge, Mass.

Lee, Laurie (1959), *Cider with Rosie*, Penguin Books, Middlesex, 1993.

—— (1969), *As I Walked Out One Midsummer Morning*, Penguin Books, Middlesex, 1993.

Lesthaeghe, Ron and Wilson, Chris (1986), 'Modes of Production, Secularization and the Pace of Fertility Decline in Western Europe, 1870–1930', in Coale and Watkins, *qv*.

Linder, Leslie (1966), *The Journal of Beatrix Potter from 1881 to 1897*, Frederic Warne, London.

Livi-Bacci, Massimo (1986), 'Social Group Forerunners of Fertility Control in Europe', in Coale and Watkins, *qv*.

Longford, Elizabeth (1964), *Victoria RI*, Weidenfeld and Nicholson, London.

Lovett, William (1876), *Life and Struggles of William Lovett*, Macgibbon and Kee, London, 1967.

Lytton, Earl of (1961), *Wilfred Scawen Blunt: A Memoir by his Grandson*, Macdonald, London.

MacFarlane, Alan (1986), *Marriage and Love in England 1300–1840*, Blackwell, Oxford.

McKeown, T. (1976), *The Modern Rise of Population*, Academic Press, New York.

—— and Record, R. G. and Turner, R. D. (1975), 'An Interpretation of the Decline of Mortality in England and Wales during the Twentieth Century', *Population Studies* 29 (3).

Malthus, Thomas (1830), 'A Summary View of the Principle of Population', *An Essay on the Principle of Population*, Penguin Books, Middlesex, 1980.

Mann, Horace (1851), *Census Report*, in Pike, *qv*.

Maugham, W. Somerset (1915), *Of Human Bondage*, Penguin Books, Middlesex, 1971.

Marchand, Leslie A. (1971), *Byron: A portrait*, John Murray, London.

Maurois, André (1953), *Leila: the Life of George Sand*, Penguin Books, London.

Mead, Edward P. (1843), in Engels, *qv*.

Meredith, George (1885), *Diana of the Crossways*, Chapman and Hall, London, 1889.

Moore, George (1894), *Esther Waters*, Penguin Books, London, 1937.

Morel, Marie-France (1991), 'Infant Mortality 1750–1914', in Schofield, Reher and Bideau, *qv*.

Morrison, Arthur (1896), *A Child of the Jago*, Penguin Books, Middlesex, 1949.

Opie, Iona and Peter (1952), *The Oxford Dictionary of Nursery Rhymes*, Clarendon Press, Oxford.

Owen, Robert Hale (1832), *Moral Physiology: or, a brief and plain treatise on the population question*.

Pike, Royston E. (1967), *Human Documents of the Victorian Golden Age*, George Allen and Unwin, London.

Place, Francis (1823), 'To the Married of Both Sexes in Genteel Life' and 'To the Married of Both Sexes of the Working People' in Teitelbaum, *qv*.

Preston, Samuel H. and Haines, Michael R. (1991), *Fatal Years: Child Mortality in Nineteenth Century America*, Princeton University Press, Princeton, NJ.

Quiggin, Pat (1988), *No Rising Generation: Women and Fertility in Nineteenth Century Australia*, Australian Family Formation Project Monograph no. 10, Department of Demography, Australian National University, Canberra.

Raleigh, Sir Walter (1616), 'Letter to his Wife on the Death of his Son', *The Oxford Book of English Prose*, University Press, Oxford, 1952.

Richardson, Henry Handel (1930), *The Fortunes of Richard Mahoney*, Penguin Books, Melbourne, 1982.

Riemer, Andrew (1992), *Inside Outside*, Angus & Robertson, Pymble.

Rose, Lionel (1986), *Massacre of the Innocents: infanticide in Great Britain 1800–1939*, Routledge & Kegan Paul, London.

Rousseau, Jean-Jaques (1762), *Emile*.

Roussel, Louis (1985), 'Le cycle de la vie familial dans le société post-industrielle', *International Population Conference, Florence*, International Union for the Scientific Study of Population, Liège.

Rowbotham, Sheila (1973), *Hidden from History*, Pluto Press, London.

Ruzicka, Lado T. and and Caldwell, John C. (1977), *The End of Demographic Transition in Australia*, Australian Family Formation Project, Monograph no. 3, Department of Demography, Australian National University, Canberra.

Saki (H. H. Munro) (1911), 'Sredni Vashtar', *The Chronicles of Clovis, The Penguin Complete Saki*, Penguin Books, London, 1982.

Schofield, Roger, Reher, David and Bideau, Alain (eds) (1991), *The Decline of Mortality in Europe*, Clarendon Press, Oxford.

Shaw, George Bernard (1916), *Pygmalion*, Penguin Books, London, 1949.

Shorter, Edward (1973), 'Female emancipation, birth control and fertility in European history', *The American Historical Review* 78 (3).

Siedlecky, Stefania and Wyndham, Diana (1990), *Populate and Perish: Australian Women's Fight for Birth Control*, Allen and Unwin, Sydney.

Smith, F. B. (1979), *The People's Health 1830–1910*, Australian National University Press, Canberra.

Sogner, Solvi (1993), 'Historical Features of Women's Position in Society', in Frederici *et al.*, *qv*.

Stratton, J. Y. (1864), in Pike, *qv*.

Stowe, Harriet Beecher (1852), *Uncle Tom's Cabin*.

Tawney, R. H. (1920), 'Preface', in Lovett, *qv*.

Taylor, A. J. P. (1965), *English History 1914–1945*, The Oxford History of England, Oxford University Press, Oxford.

Teitelbaum, Michael S. (1984), *The British Fertility Decline: Demographic Transition in the Industrial Revolution*, Princeton University Press, Princeton, NJ.

Thackeray, William Makepeace (1847), *Vanity Fair*, Pan Books, London, 1967.

Trevelyan, G. M. (1942), *English Social History*, Penguin Books, Middlesex, 1974.

Trollope, Anthony (1857), *Barchester Towers*, New English Library, London, 1963.

—— (1858), *Doctor Thorne*, Pan, London, 1968.

—— (1859), *The Bertrams*, Dover, New York 1986.

—— (1863), *Rachel Ray*, Dover, New York 1980.

—— (1867), *The Last Chronicle of Barset*, Penguin Books, Middlesex, 1967.

—— (1867), *The Claverings*, Dover, New York, 1977.

—— (1869), *He Knew He Was Right*, Oxford University Press, Oxford, 1985.

—— (1869), *Phineas Finn*, Oxford University Press, Oxford, 1969.

—— (1870), *The Vicar of Bullhampton*, Oxford University Press, Oxford, 1963.

—— (1873), *The Eustace Diamonds*, Oxford University Press, Oxford, 1968.

—— (1875), *The Way We Live Now*, Panther Books, London, 1969.

—— (1876), *The Prime Minister*, Oxford University Press, Oxford, 1968.

—— (1877), *The American Senator*.

—— (1878), *Is He Popenjoy?*.

—— (1879), *John Caldigate*.

—— (1879), *Cousin Henry*, Oxford University Press, Oxford, 1987.

—— (1881), *Dr Wortle's School*.

—— (1882), *The Duke's Children*, Oxford University Press, Oxford, 1963.

—— (1883), *An Autobiography*.

Tuchman, Barbara (1966), *The Proud Tower*, Hamish Hamilton, London.

—— (1981) *Practising History*, Macmillan, London, 1982.
van der Walle, Francine (1986), 'Infant Mortality and the European Demographic Transition', in Coale and Watkins, *qv*.
Wall, Richard (1983), 'Introduction', in Wall, Robin, n.d., Laslett, *qv*.
—— and Robin, Jean and Laslett, Peter (eds) (1983) *Family Forms in Historic Europe*, Cambridge University Press, Cambridge.
Ware (1979), 'Social Influences on Fertility at Later Ages of Reproduction', Special Supplement on Fertility in Middle Age', *Journal of Biosocial Sciences*.
Watkins, Susan Cotts (1986), 'Conclusions', in Coale and Watkins, *qv*.
Wells, Robert V. (1980), 'Illegitimacy and bridal pregnancy in colonial America', in Laslett, Oosterveen and Smith, *qv*.
White, J. Edward (1864), 'Report upon the Metal Manufacturers of the Birmingham District', in Pike, *qv*.
Wilde, Oscar (1895), *The Importance of Being Earnest*, Heinemann, London 1960.
Woodham-Smith, Cecil (1951), *Florence Nightingale*, Fontana Books, 1964.
Woods, R. I. (1987), 'Approaches to the Fertility Transition in Victorian England', *Population Studies* 41 (2).
—— and Smith, C. W. (1983), 'The Decline of Marital Fertility in the Late Nineteenth Century', *Population Studies* 37 (2).
—— and Watterson, P. A. and Woodward J. H. (1988 and 1989), 'The Causes of Rapid Infant Mortality Decline in England and Wales, 1861–1921, Parts I and II', *Population Studies* 42 (3) and 43 (1).
Wordsworth, William (1807), 'Ode on Intimations of Immortality from Recollections of Early Childhood', *The Oxford Book of English Verse*, Oxford University Press, Oxford, 1939.
—— (1807), 'My heart leaps up', *A Book of English Poetry*, Penguin, Middlesex, 1950.
—— (1807), 'Upon Westminster Bridge', *The Oxford Book of English Verse*, Oxford University Press, Oxford, 1939.
Wrigley, E. A. and Schofield, R. S. (1981), *The Population History of England*, Edwin Arnold, London.
—— (1983), 'English Population History from Family Reconstitution: Summary Results 1600–1799', *Population Studies* 37 (2).

Subject Index

Author Index

170